The Keeper of Me

a memoir

Lynn Schriner

Little Cottage Publishing

Little Cottage Publishing

The Keeper of Me
Copyright© 2015 by Lynn Schriner

This title is also available as a Little Cottage Publishing eBook.

Requests for information should be addressed to:
Little Cottage Publishing, P.O. Box 1036, Palmer Lake, CO 80133

Library of Congress Cataloging-in-Publication Data

Schriner, Lynn 1955-
    The Keeper of Me: a memoir / Lynn Schriner
    Includes bibliographical references (p.128)
    ISBN 978-0-578-17199-9 (paperback)
        1Christian life. 2. Schriner, Lynn, 1955-. 3. Religious Aspects-Life lessons-Christianity 1. Title.
Library of Congress Control Number: 2015919244
Little Cottage Publishing, Palmer Lake, CO

All Scripture quotations, unless otherwise indicated, are taken from the *Holy Bible: New International Version®* copyright © 1973, 1978, 1984 by International Bible Society

All rights reserved. No part of this publication may be reproduced, stored in a retrieval system, or transmitted in any form or by any means—electronic, mechanical, photocopy, recording, or any other—except for brief quotations in printed reviews, without prior written permission of the publisher.

Cover design: Lynn Schriner
Cover Photo: Dreamstime®
Interior design: Joe Schriner
Printed in the United States of America

To my cowboy

My sister

My dad

You three are my touchstones.

Dear Reader

When I started this book my intention was to give it as a gift to my friends and family. This book is very intimate, but after sharing it with some people, their response was, it needed to be shared with a much larger audience. I began to view the definition of family, and realized my family is the family of God, and they are all around the world. Because this may be our first time together, I wanted to catch you up on a few things.

In 2000, I wrote a book entitled "Bent, Not Broken", which is similar to this one, in which I also wrote about my suffering. At that point, it was with cancer, and the loss of one of my dear childhood friends in the plane that hit the Pentagon on 9/11. I was also being stalked by a Satanist who had moved in next door.

My life has never been easy, and my outlet has often been to write about it. Much of what you are reading will be from my journals and blogs during those times of intense trials.

During those painful years leading up to the first book, I began my ministry to help orphans in Africa. My eyes opened to their needs, and God raised up a foundation to orphans called "Damascus Ministries". I began to use my speaking and singing voice, to raise funds and awareness for their plight. So when you read about water projects; that is what I am referring to, and when you read about record producers, the music is also part of the journey. God has blessed me with some great musicians and producers. In 2013 I won Independent Country Music Association's "Folk Artist of the Year," for my project "Lynn Schriner, Amazed." As of fall 2015, with the help from the music, we have funded 15 water wells and have fed an estimated 4000 children.

My husband and I have been forced to move, over eight times since that first book was written, because of the sensitivities I have to herbicides like Roundup, and to pesticides. So much of my journey has been fighting poisoned air. It has been forty years of fighting the silent enemies in the air we breathe, after a massive pesticide hit in the late seventies, and a "perfect storm" of vaccinations to travel overseas, combined with withdrawal from the prescription drug Valium, all of which damaged my liver. This "cocktail," created the road I have been forced to travel on. In the midst of it all, I have fought hard to live and I have been shown over and over again, what enables one to live fully alive, is gratitude and grace.

The sequence of the stories are not perfect, but the message throughout is the same. GRACE. I am grateful for the daily little gifts. Life is precious and beautiful.

I pray you will become more aware of the poisons in your world. From the hairspray, to the plastic wrap, from perfume to our cleaning products. If we can change some of our habits in our own homes, it will have a great impact on our health and the health of those around us. My prayer is that you will find courage as you read my story. Courage to face your own giants without fear. I hope you will come a visitor, and leave, a friend. I hope you will see a GOD who will never leave you, and sense *his* love as you read my story. If these words move you, please let me know. I love hearing how God works in the lives of others.

Blessings and peace,

Lynn

The rooster is crowing outside my window in the deep pockets of night. There is a crazy, crescent moon and there are stars so lush, wide and all consuming, they seem to swallow me in the night. I sit out under them wrapped in wool and slippers. I am a weary traveler of sleepless, a seeker for a pocket of grace in a world gone wild. A world that gives evil and violence top billing on the evening news, while a thousand stories of grace are happening all around us and are never heard. We are continually fed the hopelessness of this world with the "Chicken Little" messages "The sky is falling! The sky is falling!" We believe this because the message is everywhere, daring us to believe. In the midst of the message, I am seeking the unending grace of God, and that *he* is still on the throne, amidst the swirling chaos.

I am in the dark, waiting for my eyes to adjust and the darkness to lift. Where light and shadow begin to exchange their created "clothing." One is shucking the cloak of darkness towards the imploding light of dawn, while another is draping on a new beginning. I am bearing witness to the exchange, and it is a daily miracle. The birds are sitting quietly amongst the branches and eves of the barn. With the switch to light, they open their mouths to sing to the Creator of all things. This amazing grace will continue to emerge as the rabbits begin quietly to eat amongst the green grasses on the prairie. A buck is resting within the grass, and slowly turns his head to sniff the breeze. I am the intimate observer of this ritual of grace amidst the noise of the morning news blasting from the television.

A change is coming to my little world. I am leaving the prairie wild with all of its raw and extreme beauty, to a quieter seclusion within the forest. I pray to settle into peace. The Lord is still on *his* throne; the same yesterday, today, and forever more, even when I have changed.

Forward

I am a firm believer that the "Lord giveth and the Lord taketh away, and blessed be the name of the Lord." Yet I grab hold of something and it is not a simple task to remove it from my hand. All the while I am believing that I am releasing it to God. God and I know the truth. I can shackle myself to my desire and, after a time of wrestling with God over the matter, fall on my knees, and cry out my need of *his* help. I am, at that point, an exhausted, cranky child. And *he*, the ever patient God.

I once placed a license plate on the back of my car with the word "VOICE" on it, because God has indeed given me a voice. It has been my blessing and it has been my trial. Words that cut, words that healed. A voice that carries Christ, a voice that goes to war. This book is my gift to God. I want these words to matter to you, the reader, but most of all I want these words to remind me of how great God is. Even when I don't understand *him*. Even when I can't hear *him*, or sense *him* near. God is good all the time. I want *him* to be present in these words, and bring them to life. Most of all I want God to know that I love *him*. There may be some words in this story of me that seem contrary to that statement. I have wandered in the wilderness of my raw and real times. Yet my heart knows that in the depths of its song, *his* love will wrap me in the words that I hear, and those words, the truth of *his* presence within my heart, will remain. *His* words cover me like a blanket with *his* grace. *He* is, above all else, the keeper of me. I am thankful.

Contents

Chapter one – After the Poisons Come / 1

Chapter two – Prairie Madness / 18

Chapter three – Crazy Love / 28

Chapter four – Gravestones / 33

Chapter five – Nine-Eleven / 37

Chapter six – Borrowed Time / 46

Chapter seven – Red Moon / 51

Chapter eight – Wanderings / 56

Chapter nine – Lone Thoughts from a High Wire / 69

Chapter ten – Earth is a School / 74

Chapter eleven – Messengers / 79

Chapter twelve – Feast of Miracles / 87

Chapter thirteen – Mission of Joy / 95

Chapter fourteen – Touchstones / 100

Chapter fifteen – Amazing Grace / 108

Chapter sixteen – Blessings / 116

Chapter seventeen – I Have Gone Round / 120

Chapter eighteen – Come Inside / 123

Chapter nineteen – Beauty for Ashes / 126

Acknowledgments / 128

Notes / 132

Bible References / 134

After Notes / 135

Venus and Mars / 136

Being authentically broken is closer to Jesus than pretending everything is okay.

Chapter one

After the Poisons Come

I was in my garden of happy endings one day at the end of summer. The little organic farm we called home for eight years was flourishing under our care. We had planted gardens for bees and hummingbirds. Baby rabbits played under the trolley that sat in the garden. People came and stayed there in the little bed & breakfast. Our horses had two acres to run and the scent of summer was drifting in the breeze. I was happy and content and praising God and thankful. I had a sweet girlfriend and her children on one side of the farm. We had an outdoor movie experience watching Cirque du Solei on a sheet under the stars. We went for walks, had bible studies, and threw parties.

The orphan work was going well, and I was recording some new material with a producer/musician in Texas. We were living in the country, in my garden of happy endings, where birds came every morning to sing me a love song. It was my safe place, a shelter that allowed me to heal from all the moves we had been forced to do.

The rancher behind us hired out a man to spray his fields. I saw him pulling a large tank behind his tractor. I watched the plumes of poisonous 2-4d* and Plateau* go upon the fields of gold. I had filmed my video for the song Dance in that beautiful field, with the rancher's amazing horses. My first thought was for the baby bunnies under the trolley. My second thought was to close the windows and to drive away. It was too late. By the time I had driven away my lungs were burning, my head was pounding, and I was nauseated and dizzy. By the second week my stomach felt like I had swallowed shattered glass. I tried to return home for five consecutive weeks. My weight plummeted from one hundred pounds to eighty-four pounds. The field they had sprayed burned with the chemical. The horses got sick and we lost our safe place, our home, that fateful day. I cried out to God in pain and anger. I couldn't breathe nor sleep, and my body was scorching hot. I was covered in red-hot fire under my skin.

I found that all the Christian platitudes that in the past had dressed me in white at the altar of *his* grace, had fallen off my body into tattered strips of nothingness, which left me gasping in the wind. For a season my faith was small.

God is still grace in the midst of my pain, no matter how far down I am. Somehow, someway, the prayers that had risen up on my behalf, like bubbles of light at heaven's floor, had drawn the face of mercy once more. I would rise from the pain and begin the journey back to life after having all the powers of hell unleashed upon me, darker than any imagined thing. When I surrendered and lay quiet, waiting to perish, with words uttering from parched and fevered lips, "I trust you God; I love you God," there wasn't another sound but for my breath. The pain lifted that night, the tide turned, and I would live.

I lost my home, my garden, my place of business and source of income. I lost my sweet Christian neighbor and the light from my window seat, where I watched the birds come every morning as I sipped my tea. That same year I lost my baby brother, Brett, my mother, and my sweet friend, Tom. I lost my security, my safety, and my trust in my fellow man. For upon hearing what had happened, the rancher said that he was "Sorry, but if I can't spray, my land is useless." The poisons killed his field, which rendered his land useless after all.

What I found in the end was God, as *he* has always been. I found *him* in the new friends for whom I am eternally thankful. They gave me shelter in the storm, opened their arms to me while I wept, made me a bed to lay my fevered head, and wept tears for me as they prayed for an end to my pain. God resided in those tears, for in their embrace, God wrapped me in *his* arms, and never let me go.

~~~

I transport my soul out of this broken body and I am seeking God with such hunger that I am tearing into *his* words like meat at a banquet table. I am a woman without a home, in a body given the keys to be my jailer. Captive behind the bars of chemicals that have snaked into every cell of my being. My stomach turns into my tormentor when I eat something as simple as apple sauce. I turn inward to the pain and moan, and shake, and cry out to God, who calls me by name, yet allows homes of our making to become useless to my need of shelter.

Stretched beyond my limits, I face the peeling paint on a

broken down garage. The prairie skies, where we have run to escape the poisons, bring in white sheets of icy layers. Tiny sparrows flit into two lonely trees and fluff up their feathers against the winds, while sheltering nesting boxes lay dormant and empty as they choose to ride out winter in the wide expanse of storms. Am I being led to ride out the storms, (from the vantage point of a branch), while the "nesting box" that my man is working tirelessly to provide for me must lay dormant and empty because my body has gone rogue? I know... from the sweat of his brow...the measure of his love for me. I know... from the bedroom, which the two people of grace have made available for me...that God has a plan. But today I feel orphaned.

~~~

It seems God had a better plan for all of us. Not necessarily to move on to that which was ours, and get on with our lives, but to learn the lessons *he* had for us (my husband, my friends, and me), that would keep us seeking *him* in higher measure.

The healing of two women, who reside in one of the women's home, will stir up, shake up, and cause them to hear their hearts cry for a closer walk with God, by looking at themselves. The women struggle to stay in peace; God's timing is not their own. Apart from the body that won't cooperate with our agenda, aside from the sharing of a bedroom in the home of fellow pilgrims searching for peace, what will God bring if we will stop wrestling with *him* to take control? We cry out for God to allow us to be servants, to be vessels of God to one another, and then wonder at *his* goodness if it is not done on our terms and on our timetable. God, who can change a dry, barren land into deep valleys of green, create the heavens and the earth, and call life into existence with a word, does *he* not know when a homeless girl should go into her home? Does the God who knows when a sparrow falls, who creates angels called Cherubim, who parts the sea so that the mysteries of a new way become clearer to the Israelites who have no home, will that God not be the guiding light to the healing that we all long for?

Wasn't the healing for Israel a collective acceptance of God's perfect will for *his* chosen people? Did those same people finally understand *his* great love when *he* parted that sea for them to pass through? While they were grumbling and looking back, God still saved them from themselves. I pray, in my pain, to stop trying to figure it all out. God's got a plan for all who are traveling, as our wayward hearts cry out, "Lord, lead me on."

~~~

I awaken empty, waiting to be filled. The sky is a wide expanse of pale blue in a winter's cloak. I am a hungry bird with my mouth wide open, calling out to be fed. My man is working hard while I must rest. He is staying out on the ranch while I am in the bedroom of our friend's home. The phone is our tether, our lifeline that binds us during this time. We are as distant as the sun is from the moon. We are both burned by the staggering losses. Our prayers are as unreliable as the phone which drops calls continually. We will be having our time of prayer, and I envision him up against the one window in the house that allows cell service (sometimes), while I lay in bed and weep. His voice will come and go... "Lord --------------- -----------loved ones------------forgive------------ -----help us-----------." I am straining to hear the longing of his heart, my hunger in the silence, and our hurting in a broken connection. God hears, I believe, the longing of our hearts. Not just the human voice, but also whispers from the soul. *He* hears, even when I cannot speak.

I so want to know God. I am watching *him*, as a mother watches her newborn baby. I am studying *him*, like one studies a lover. I look out to the new day, waiting to be filled by the *creator* and *his* created. What was God thinking when *he* created that amazing swell of prairie hill overlooking mountains that stretch closer to *him?* Or the moon, so low upon the fields that it covers the expanse of my eyes on the horizon? So perfectly round and beckoning, as the sun comes from the east and the world is turning on its axis, calling gently to all living beings to rise and go about their days. I draw nearer to God through *his* created forms of beauty, *his* glory calling out from this amazing tapestry of life called planet earth.

~~~

God, creator of heaven and earth, the skies, and every living thing, of which I am one, how can I continually draw from the well of your glory? When often times I am in the valley of dry bones, your word says for me to "Prophesy to these bones to hear the word of the Lord." *

And, "I will put breath in you and you will come to life. Then you will know that I am the Lord."

I look around me and I begin to see all of heaven in every created being. I feel *his* presence in the birds that raise up their hearts and voices to sing in the dark, in trees that bend in the wind calling out *his* name, in all creatures great and small who live in knowing *his* instinctual directive for their lives.

~~~

Where in this barren landscape of wind-tossed prairie do I bring glory to God? I have no hearth or home. No child has ever been born to this broken hearted woman, or has ever nursed at her breast. No tangible measure of God's tender nod of approval in the normal ways of life.

Within this season of loss and poisons, my beloved man and I are venomous with words that strike one another again and again. Why do we say these things to one of God's precious creations? How can we move through our losses and pain, to be filled once again? This pain, these losses, have seemingly driven out heavenly light as surely as the storm clouds cover the sun through the deepest of winter, as my man and I are slinging arrows at one another. Battling one another as if we are the enemy, and all I can think of is why? Why can't we be filled with enough of our creator, our heaven, our God, to be the hands and feet of Christ to one another and to others, beyond this windblown, barren time of storm and winter? Why do we land repeatedly into the breaking of glass hearts that we have called home? How does one's face go from beloved to the enemy? How will God change the twisting of the knife in my guts, to a balm of healing water? From torn to tender, in the blink of an eye?

"Fill me Lord!" I cry from my curled up child who lives within me. The shame, the blame, the endless conversations about right and wrong. Suddenly I have been laid to waste, as if the poison liquids and fumes were a tsunami, not only devastating the landscape of my internal function, but also laying bare the wrongs of my man and me. Still the sun rises and falls and this day is set before me. It's the only one I know for sure I will have, and my choice is to see with eyes that are love, God's love, if I am not able to find my own. To shift the understanding and perspective in this storm, so that I can see this man (who is normally kind), and see his gifts and remember his value in God's eyes. Let me remember all the gifts in this season of what has been lost; hot water, sight to see birds feeding, a bed to rest upon, and music I can hear. God is everywhere. *He* is singing, humming, illuminating the most simple of gifts, and showing *his* love. I will turn my eyes upward to *his* light and remember from where my help comes.

~~~

When circumstances come crashing in upon our heads year after year, with losses piling so high upon our dreams for a good life, that it breaks off a large part of our foundation we call grace, when sisters are born without the ability to connect, when brothers grow old and die at a young age, when death buries hope, when neighbors become hissing vessels of evil, and life is narrowed by bent wreckage, there seems to be no light at the end of the tunnel. Only blood, broken bones, shattered hearts, and seemingly endless desires for something else remains.

I hear from the word and from the pulpit to "thank the Lord in all things." So I do. For all things, both great and small. Then somewhere the devil dances, it seems, and all is lost. A home, health, a marriage, a friendship, a loved one. And we sit in the ashes of our lives and God becomes, at best, indifferent. When mercy seems like an elusive morsel held high above a starving soul, where is the safety, the joy, or the stability?

When the ground is shifting, and the world as we have known it has shattered, God, my redeemer and the lifter of my head, suddenly seems to not care of what I have lost.

Across the street, the neighbor's field of life is ripe and bursting with blessing, while our fields are dry, barren and scorched. I can close my heart to the only one who can save me while I have eyes only to see the suffering. From the orphans in Africa, to the suffering of animals and children around the world, to innocence lost. I am listening to the lisping lie that says "God would never do this to someone *he* loves." So I cry out from my heap of ashes, "What did I do that you should punish me like this?" I become the prophet of old who says "Take my life." Yet even that harsh word, left hanging through the pain in the air, seems to not move God. *He* appears as indifferent as the wind blowing ice across the barren land. My heart closes with the raw, oozing wounds of pain and loss, and it becomes my truth. God is mad. *He* is mad at all of us! *He* must be! Look all around at the suffering everywhere while an indifferent God watches. We have thrown God out of our schools, government, marriages, child bearing, and lands. Surely all the suffering, the losses, the school shootings, the "right-is-wrong" mentality, the shattered-glass feeling in my stomach, the yelling in my home, the loss of income, must mean I am, we are, forsaken. God is mad! "Why are you punishing me?" I cry out. "How can I trust a God like that?"

~~~

I am driving the long two-hour drive from my weekly doctor's appointment and I am reflecting on the news from the doctor. I have ulcerated colitis and a bruised spine. The herbicide has injured my kidneys and my liver, and they are shutting down. My blood sugars are up and down, the infection loads in my body are rampant. My brother is nearing the end of his life in hospice, and there is another school shooting this morning. As tears are flowing from my weary and burning eyes, a Jeep pulls in front of me and stops. On the back window in bold letters

I see the words *God is not mad at you.* What? I look again, unsure of what I am seeing. *God is not mad at you.* I sit in the black car with my lack of understanding wrapping me in shadowed angst, as the sun is passed by clouds, covering its glory.

The light changes and the Jeep goes flying off. I begin to chase the Jeep to see who is driving and to call out "Hey, did God tell you I was here?" All eighty-six pounds of pain? If God is not mad at me, the hurting, cloudy spirit of me, masked in all the layers of "why,"- then how do I let go of my need to understand, and how does all this evil suddenly become grace?

As I chase the Jeep I see that behind the wheel is a girl, all tats and dyed-black hair, with the window down on a cold and gray day. She is smiling. She turns her head to the sudden streak of light, and I rise up in my seat wanting to ask, "How do you know? How do you know God is not mad at me?"

This tattooed girl, with the bumper sticker gospel, puts the pedal to the metal and is gone from my sight in record time. I slowly turn for my temporary home stunned, with the Band-Aid gospel message that has been laid across my broken heart. I know that somehow I have just been christened with the truth of God's heart for me. This wandering, lost sojourner of why, knows in that moment, that *his* touch cracked open the shadowed lie that I have believed, and I, who have begged for *his* touch, am suddenly lighter with the truth. The sun breaks at long last through the clouds and the light places a tender touch of love from God upon my cheek, and I am humbled. God is not mad at me. In that instant I know *he* is who he says *he* is and I am covered in *his* grace.

~~~

Between the Stars I Listen

If I speak softly will I be heard?
I can hide in my thicket of thoughts
Hold my tongue, twist the words
Or better still make no sound at all.
I am captured, flung into his heavens,
Between stars I listen,
Is that you God coming round the bend in the universe?
Will I see those who have crossed over now?
Abraham, Martin, and John?

Kenny, Tom, and Rich,

A brother named Brett, a Grandmother named Georgia,

My beloved furry friends who saved my life.

Time and memory rock me, like a baby in your arms,

I know too much; I see too little. God, is that your wink

Behind the moon? Take me beyond the day and night.

I will not fight you anymore, knocking on your gated

door, the guard is love.

The clock strikes midnight,

You're dance of grace begins.

I am a lonely sojourner; you, my only friend.

Chapter two

Prairie Madness

On the prairie, on the wild prairie, I learned to take a seat. I learned to hold my words, as the wind would carry them away without being heard. I learned to lean in and not fight the forces that will render me speechless. I learned to work when it was sleeping, and rest when it was wailing. Like a woman in labor, I learned to breathe between the waves of pain that tore across the grass and took away my dreams.

~~~

In the house, the prairie house, is a man who calls me his girl. He toils and works to bring a better life for me. I am the bearer of his frustration. I know this and I am sorry, but my body is not listening to my desire, not able to move into the house that is unfinished. There are too many chemicals and mold spores for my cells to say yes. So I live out in a thirty-six foot moving wonder, complete with a kitchen and a bath. It is sheltering me from the house that makes me rash, my stomach cramp and turn to glass if I stay too long. I am thankful for it all. But in the whipping, punishing wind that takes my breath and my voice and throws them to the next county over, I lose heart to revisit grace. This has been a punishing year. I lay at night under the stars and listen to the choir of frogs in the distance. They mesmerize me, this symphony of stars and frogs. I drift in sleep and abruptly come to awareness as the flashes of loves lost come parading before my eyes. A mother I was never close to, a brother that was an addict, a friend who was one of my dearest. The chemical spraying took my home, my health and my dreams in one sweeping day. I am on the prairie in isolation, stunned and often staggering around in the dust and the huge expanse of nothingness, weeping. I long for the distraction of city noises, but I cannot live there anymore. My body is broken from the modern weapons of war on the health of the planet and its created beings. With names like "Roundup," from companies like Monsanto, Bayer, Johnson and Johnson, and Dow chemical. There is a book I read in high school, "Silent Spring" by Rachel Carson (who was deemed a fanatic in her time), and the images she wrote about, come flooding back to me. I am living her vision of death and suffering. Much like a permanent scar, I cannot safely breathe any of the chemicals released, sprayed and used on a daily basis. The masses of people are choosing to buy the lies that these chemical companies spin in their million dollar campaigns. Lies meant to manipulate our minds to believe the chemicals are safe. *Not safe.* Not for babies, or bees, or birds. Not safe for cancer survivors, or those who are struggling with depression. Not safe for ground water, or the oceans or lungs that need fresh air!

I grew up in an affluent neighborhood where spraying happened on a daily or weekly basis. My first depression happened to me after walking home from junior high one day. One minute I am happy and full of energy; the next minute I am walking through where a lawn care company is spraying the weeds. I arrived home feeling absolutely beside myself and vomited. I became very depressed overnight.

Over the years of reading and educating myself on chemicals I found these to be classic symptoms of poisoning. Headaches out of nowhere, feeling like you have the flu, unexplained anger. It's all symptoms of toxicity. It was the beginning of the hell that I have come to know.

My mom lived in that affluent neighborhood for over fifty years. She suffered from neurological symptoms (much like Parkinson's) and she died from cancer. She lived in the midst of beauty, and poisons, and they killed her. Cancer is not pretty. Her death was better than most but I am still haunted by her final hours. The neighborhood she lived in is full of stories of people dying with cancer.

I bolt upright in my bed and am forced to listen to my heart pounding. I wrench open the door to move out under the stars, and hear the quiet in the wide open spaces. This is not what I have prayed for. These losses, this pain, the "sentencing" to live in wide open spaces, in an RV next to a home that is uninhabitable, as my man sleeps in a bed alone because I am in too much pain to share mine. Life is a mystery. God is not defined by any sort of reasoning with *him* to change me. *He* is strangely quiet, while I am a half mad woman living on the prairie, with the wind whipping her hair across her face like a weapon.

I will sit here, long after the moon has crossed the sky, listening, straining to hear from God. Does *he* not wish to answer me in the longing cry of my heart?

Is *his* silence a storm, which I am in the eye of? For it's in the in-between of trials that my madness occurs. Walking country roads, sobbing my heart out as bewildered calves look over at me with sad eyes. There is no one else to hear the tears. Only quiet in the open spaces.

I will return to sanity I know. One day the punishing winds will stop. One day the flowers and the green of the valley will rise from the prairie brown. One day I will hear a still small voice call my name and the memory of those gone will bring a smile and not a tear. One day the quiet of the open spaces will ease my heart. I sit in the dirt and I wait.

~~~

As a prairie chick, I am learning to get up before dawn and begin my walk. I can see the tiny lights of Jupiter and Mars on the horizon. I can hear the sounds of cattle and deer rustling in the forest trees and animals foraging by moonlight. I find myself often having long chats with God as I walk in the dawn's early light. I have chosen to listen to the chatter in my mind. It's quite the jumbled up mess I must confess. The Bible says we have the mind of Christ. I am pretty sure the Savior of the world doesn't think like me. I am amazed at the negativity that comes from within me. Surely the thoughts that ramble through mine need to be censored. I can't have two positive thoughts in a row without getting a brain cramp! I understand that a lot of the thoughts that have taken up residence in my mind are from grief and loss. Depression is not a positive bedfellow. I need to cut me some slack I guess. But honestly I am blaming most of these wild thoughts on the wind. Not the gentle breezy type of a summer wind, no, this is the whip you senseless kind of a prairie wind. The grit in your eyes, push you down, take your feet out from under you, throws stock tanks across the prairie landscape kind. The kind of wind that slams into your house and bangs on everything that is not nailed securely down. The kind that takes a part of your roof and leaves it a quarter of a mile down the road. I have had a lot of time thinking about the wind since I moved out onto the barren prairie. My first thought (after picking myself up off the ground) is "What did I do to make God mad?" But then I thought "No, don't take this personally." I am pretty sure the wind has been a factor out in this forsaken land for a really long time. Just ask the poor prairie gals who came before me. Pioneer women, with a lot more to complain about, I am sure. I am pretty sure they were privy to their own thoughts that were driving them slowly mad. I believe they called it "Prairie Madness". I seem to have picked up the mad part. I am a city girl gone wild.

~~~

I used to live in the land of what's next? What is going to happen tomorrow? Will I get a phone call that could change my life? What if I get that record deal or get to be on that television program, will the public hear it? If I rent this hotel ballroom for a fundraiser will it be worth it? Am I doing enough, who is going to die next?

One day, in the middle of the day, for no particular reason, I flipped that switch off. I started looking around me, at the light coming through the window, at the colors in the fields. I began noticing the smell of my husband's skin. I started living in the here and now, in a new and different way. It has changed me to do so. I see the moon every night and I give thanks. I see the hawk fly from the trees and I give thanks. I talk to my beloved dad and I give thanks. I experience my life fully, without filters, in the moment of the experience. I want to be fully alive. I want to live while I am alive. To awaken each day to a new life. To understand the gift given. These gifts are not guarantees. I can't justify living carelessly.

   I see God all around me now, from the tiniest of creatures on the leaves in my garden, to the incredible sweeping glory of a full moon in the prairie sky. I am kneeling under the stars of creation and I am the shepherd boy, David, in the field thousands of years ago. I am a witness to God's hand today. *His* continuing presence of *his* glory. I can be thankful now, in this moment, after the Tsunami of circumstances tried to remove my blessings. I am reminded, with each breath, of the reason to keep fighting the good fight. Life is beautiful, even when it breaks your heart, even when it cracks your soul, even when you fear the worst. God is this timeless infinite love, so far above my understanding, the Creator of heaven and earth, and the divine Creator of me. I am tiny in the story. *He* deserves the glory.

Prairie Wild

I am the prairie wild

I am the wind that blows

I am the sad eyed cow in the field

I am the gentle breath of my horse that knows.

I am lonely in the wild lands

I am carried by the winds

I am held by Gods hands

A child once again.

The love cries out each morning

It gently calls my name

I am the one who listens

I am the one who choses blame.

God you are the one who loves me

In your deep and mysterious ways

And I, a stumbling sojourner

Begging for your grace,

A teacher and a truant

I am the river wild,

I know you are my way through it

Selah...I will pause.... Amen

Chapter three

Crazy Love

He hands me this earth, this day, this life and *he* says "Run with it! Share it! Give it out! Like the loaves and the fishes, there is much more here than meets the eye. Do not be afraid to embrace this day. Do not be afraid to give it away!"

I remember the scene in the movie "Oliver", where the orphan comes up with his empty bowl and begs "Please sir, may I have some more?" Why am I always wanting more? Why can't I trust that *he* will provide for me? I am much like a squirrel with my seeds, nuts and berries. I am constantly trying to accumulate more and hide them in the base of a tree or a closet or a bank. I count the numbers in my head, will I have enough? To do what? Retire? Pay bills? Take care of my health? What am I afraid of? I am trying to fund our 15th * water well as I write this. I have the money in the savings account to finish the fundraising efforts, but I am holding back. My husband's jobs have not been able to pay the bills for a while and the savings account is going down. I am unable to work anymore so who will take care of things if I give the savings away? Surely God will bring the rest of the money for these beautiful children through someone else who is healthy and working...right? But month after month there is no movement to help me fund this well, and the eight hundred dollars that remains to fund it is sitting in a bank unused because I am afraid to trust. I am the beggar with the bowl. I have given a good chunk of money to the well already, why won't anyone else help me? I remember my mother, who sat in front of a television program for hours, watching the stock markets go up and down. Her moods changed with the numbers on the screen and her anxiety seeped deeply into my childish misunderstanding of money. I absorbed her needs into my cells, her feelings of lack, her fears of releasing. I bore her fears and I carry them still. Fear of loss, even though we lived with plenty. Fear of the well running dry. If I look at my feelings about money, I see my beggar mentality. My inability to release to God everything I have and everything I am. I remember the bible story of the rich man who hoarded his wealth. God said he was foolish and *he* called him home that very night. His money meant nothing. Money is not for us to capture and bury, it is to be given. Generously and without calling it back in. I have an example of that with my dad. While my mother was fearful, my dad has always been generous and open. He has given and given and given of his money and his time and his skills to others, and God has continued to take care of him. His well has never run dry. He has been given friendships and honor and love. He has been able to travel as much as he has desired. He has been blessed with good health and energy way into his eighties. He is by all accounts a blessed man. I want to be more like my dad. I always have. But most especially I want to be more like Jesus. *He* gave of *his* entire life to others. *He* doesn't say "You owe me." *He* just says "*Trust me.*" *He* never rejects me after I have wandered long away from *him*. *His* arms just open, *his* love heals. I have to let go to be able to receive. *He* is always there. So I am going to release that money… I can let go. I can trust. I know that in giving we receive *his* joy. It's been a repeat lesson of grace for me. I open my hand

and *he* takes it in *his*. I release my fear and *he* takes it. I drink of *his* cup and I am strengthened. I give of the stock pile of goods from the blessings of my life and it becomes a river of living water to a dry and barren land for children without fresh water. I can accept this grace and I am thankful for the joy. I matter, they matter. We are all connected those children and us. There is no separation in the light of God's love. *He* is the vine and we are the branches.

Orphan Cry

I want to see the girl I love,
Skippin on the streets
Instead of a child with no shoes on,
Without enough to eat
And I want to sing to you again,
Remind you of the shape we're in
And help bring suffering to an end,
Every orphans cry.
Every child deserves a voice,
Every life deserves to shine,
And every babe should have a choice,
To live as if their mine.
No Child should be alone,
No child should have no home,
In a dry and barren land they roam,
I hear every orphan's cry. *

"Orphan Cry" from the CD Lynn Schriner, Amazed

Chapter four

Gravestones

The sky hangs low upon the mountain. There is a remnant of yesterday's memories clinging to the breath of me. I am holding my breath, waiting for a pregnant pause to open a deluge of tears upon her gravestone. I am sensing her loss rising up from my festering grief. I hear a hummingbird rushing past me and I go down to my knees. A black crow in the forest tree cries out, mocking me, while the strains of minor chords in my head transport the tears out of my heart. I hear the wailing and I begin to shake. I am raw and wild in my grief. I am sobbing on the mountains edge and I am in blindness and without skin, as she lays still as death beneath the piles of mountain stones that mark her passing. I am here, in my story, carrying the weight of ash cloth upon my burdened back. I sense the complete weariness of loss as I fix my gaze upon the pain. The rain begins to fall upon my uplifted face as God's tears are mingling with my own and I can hear Christ on the cross as *he* cries out "My God, my God why has thou forsaken me?" Oh yes, *he* knows the pain of giving *his* all for those ungrateful souls, of which I am one. I am fixating on my losses while forgetting *his* sacrifice for me, that I might have life instead of crying out for death. Clawing my way to the grave in my bitterness and sorrow, bound by deaths sting until the heavenly rains come to soak my clothing, I am wandering in *his* love...redeeming me. I am small and broken and *he* is... *He* is the rain, the moon, the sun, the stars, the cross, the miracles, the Holy, the Christ. *HE* is the light of day and *he* could remove the stones from her grave. I sense a stillness and remember the words in the Bible as those left behind searched for *his* body. "Who are you looking for? *He* has risen just as *he* said *he* would." said the angel at the garden tomb. Bewildered, the band of believers stumble home processing the truth of the tomb, just as *he* said it would be. The Savior lives and it is appointed once for us to die.

In the aftermath of my tears she lays still, but I have risen. She is gone and I am alive. I raise my eyes in the rain, collecting the tears of grace cascading down my face. The earth calls to heaven, while light comes gently down, reminding me to notice all that lives. Every created thing; grass, birds, light and heart will praise him, every cry, tear and sigh speaks *his* name. I can choose to be lost in the after math of so many deaths, one right after the other, or I can choose to know that death has no sting when we trust the words our Savior spoke from the cross as he released his spirit. "It is finished." I am still alive, against all odds. He wants me to live. I rise from the ground and dry my eyes and ready myself to finish my race. One day I will see all those I loved. One day we will sit together and break the bread and pick up the baby and embrace the dogs that went before us. I taste the sweet of those words on my tongue and notice all the tears have left me. It's only gratitude and grace that will carry me. The rain stops and the light begins to rise through the mist. As do I, walking back to sanity, no longer adrift.

~~~

Lay It Down

There are so many lost
Kneeling by the grave
Kiss the ground, afraid
The beloved fits inside a heart
As they leave our sight
We carry them forever—
Neither heavy nor light.
I see shadows now
Where once they were the sun,
I hear their hearts whisper
"I'm free, I'm home, it is done"
Lay it down.
Nothing is forever
See you later,
Love that never dies
See you later.
Oh death where is your sting?
Every created thing must die
Lay it down.

Chapter five

Nine Eleven

She was my north for a good part of my formative years, a compass and a map of what to do and how to be. I feel lost without her, though we had drifted apart by miles and marriage and babies. We talked sometimes on the wire sharing our ghosts and our joys, hanging up believing our paths would connect again. There was always time she would say, "Next summer."

The sanctuary is filled to the brim with tears. There are four candles burning in a box of sand. Charlie, Leslie, Dana and Zoe. There is no room to breathe, there is so much pain, so much loss. A family, my friends. Her dear friend Judy looks at me with ragged eyes, "Oh Lynn!" she cries. I hold her hand and our tears are like tributaries into a collective river of grief going out to sea.

~~~

I am fighting cancer. It is dark and ravenous. I am doing cancer treatments alone while my man is living away working, and my sister/friend, has moved away. I have written a book and it has been published, celebrated and shared with the media. The cancer treatments are so painful I am screaming and rocking, naked, in a bath tub. A friend calls to check on me and when she hears my pain, she says "I am coming" She comes and sits beside me and holds my hand. She is grace in my suffering and she does not flinch.

This grace came when words and my breath have left me. There are no words for this kind of grace. Her tears were *his*. Her hand squeezing mine was *his*.

~~~

One morning there is a phone call from Chicago with a request to be interviewed on a Christian television station the following Tuesday morning. I stare down at my leg with a hole in it (from the cancer) and the crutches that are holding me together like the straw man in the Wizard of Oz and I say "Yes, I will come" My man who has been AWOL in all ways that mattered during this time, agrees to fly with me. I have not flown in ten years and I do not fly lightly. My fears of flying and being out of control have magnified since nine eleven. I find myself, on the day of our flight, grasping his hand and crying, my heart slamming in my chest like a rocket ship about to launch. My man is the exact opposite of me, finding bliss in things that bring terror to most, and thriving on adventure. We have problems with our connecting flight and rent a car instead. We drive past grazing horses that make me smile for the first time in weeks. We arrive at the hotel which has been paid for us. The driver from the TV station comes the next morning and drives us to the studio where we meet a former Miss America who is interviewing me. I am sitting in the make-up chair, the lights accentuating my dark circles and struggles with the cancer treatments. I feel lost and not centered. As I pray, it appears that God is listening to someone else, because my prayers feel like they have never left the room. When the interview begins, I feel as far away as the cameraman off set. I feel like I am failing, and the audience is off getting another cup of coffee rather than listen this drivel of a woman carry on. My man is off-set, smiling encouragingly towards me, and Miss America's sweet face is trying to prod me to say something of importance while my mind has gone to mush. The interview ends as I deflate and the grip comes to remove the microphone from my jacket and says something like "Thank you" But in my state of mind it sounds more like "Thank God that's over!"

We walk off, my man and I, when suddenly the former Miss America and two other women come and say they feel led to pray for us. I am thinking, I bet! Is it that obvious that we are losers at this Christianity thing? Our marriage is fractured, my health is hanging by a thread and I can't even say anything anointed, for Pete's sake, when given the opportunity by God. So they gather around us, lay their hands upon us and begin to pray. I don't remember the exact words, but the message was one of love, encouragement and strength. Our bodies and spirits lifted in the love, we left with the driver back to the hotel and then off to the airport for our flight home.

We are standing in the Chicago O'Hare Airport and the terminal is packed with chaos. We stand shoulder to shoulder in line after line of weary, frightened and stressed people, waiting, because overworked airport and homeland security agents are going over each one of us with a fine toothed comb. There are babies crying, teenagers arguing and I am praying a lot because the rocket ship is starting to fire up again in my chest, while an airport employee is talking over a little loud speaker, telling people to remove their shoes and hats and be ready to remove their coats. I am trying to figure out how I am going to sneak my water bottle onto the plane when the Lord whispers to me, "*You are going to sing to these people.*" I look around at the hundreds, maybe thousands, of people in this chaos around me and think, what? Just then, the man with the microphone is asking if anyone wants to sing a song. He looks across the room of multitudes, and seeing my man in his cowboy hat, says into the loud speaker

"Hey cowboy, where you from?" My man glances around then points to himself. "Yea you, where you from cowboy?"

Dipping his head, my man says "Colorado" I am still trying to process what God's message to me was and how in the world I was going to do that, when I see the man with the microphone walking towards my man.

"Hey cowboy" he says, "Wanna sing us a song?"

I hear my man say "I don't sing, but she does." and he points to me. The man looks over at me, with the rocket ship going off in my chest, and asks,

"You want to sing us a song?"

I nod and say "Yea, I guess I do." He hands me the microphone and I close my eyes. In the span of a minute, I have been given a directive from God to sing to *his* people. I open my mouth and out comes the sweetest sound. "Amazing grace, how sweet the sound, that saved a wretch like me. I once was lost, but now I'm found, was blind, but now I see…" The entire concourse goes silent, every baby stops crying, and every argument ceases. The notes fly out of my mouth and up into the heights of this cavernous concourse and it sounds like Carnegie Hall through this one tiny, little speaker. All movement has paused. "Through many dangers, toils and snares, we have already come. T'was grace that brought us here thus far and grace will lead us home." You could hear a pin drop. "When we've been there, ten thousand years, bright shining as the sun, we've no less days, to sing God's praise, as when we first begun." People are wiping their eyes and weeping softly. "Amazing grace, how sweet the sound, that saved a wretch like me. I once was lost, but now I'm found, was blind, but now I see…" The last note suspends in the air and when it falls silent, there is a pregnant pause of glory, and then the applause begins. The smiles and laughter and the peace of God falls upon *his* people. There is no more fear or pain, because God sent this gift, *his* holy symphony, to serenade the wounded hearts, and there is glory in the house.

As movement resumes, we clear through the security check point and board the plane. All around us we hear people talking about what just happened.

"Did you hear that?" I hear them asking each other from all sides. I sit down next to my man, and on his other side, next to the window, sits a girl. She asks us if we heard the singing.

"Yes" my man replies, "It was my wife."

She looks at me and says, "I have never heard anything like that before." and then says softly, "I am afraid to fly." I reach across my man and offer her his hand.

"Here, you can borrow him for a bit if you like, it helps." She took his hand as I took his other hand, and we flew into the night, sharing the message of Jesus to her broken soul. As dusk fell to darkness, in the silence of hushed voices on the plane, she found some light.

No Hate

Rendered, wrenched, torn and broken

We wandered,

We wept,

We rose,

We prayed,

We trembled,

Mixed tears and blood

Cracked hate,

Found love too late-

We ache for home

For a safe place to be protected-

We will not forget

We will hold it to our bosom

Tell our stories

Forgive

That we might live

Chapter six

Borrowed Time

And so we live on borrowed time.

Life creates beautiful illusions for the desperate soul. The illusions call out from behind the grocery store displays of dead food in pretty packaging that does not nourish life but will eventually destroy its quality. Illusion walks by in the forms of men and women objectified. The illusion's that life is fair, and we are nothing without our looks, and evil corporations in America are looking out for our best interest. We are told lies of GMOs, red dyes and thirty-eight grams of sugar are "not so bad." We live day-in and day-out with illusions that bad things will not happen to us. That all the years of choices to smoke or drink or eat fast foods won't create suffering, or early death.

The rains fall on the just and the unjust, the harsh winds blow, the flood waters rise, and we rail at the injustice of it all. We have made choices, not babies, and now we feel alone. We spoke our truths to clear our souls and expected to find peace. Instead we watched loved ones walk out the door. We have the illusion that we are somehow immune to the choices we have made. The day-to-day choices of dessert over vegetables, of sitting in fear under blankets of doubt instead of having faith. We made choices of justifying our bad behaviors and calling it "being human," and we stand outside our lives and look in, all the while waiting for the blessings to come. What if this is the day of blessing, while being dressed as a beggar instead of the King? What if we are sitting one day in the doctor's office and their mouth is telling us that our time has come and there is nothing more to be done; or we are crossing the road that we have crossed every morning, and a texting driver slams into our bodies, will our last thought on this earth be "I'm not ready!" Truth be told, today is the time that matters, the ticking of today's clock, right here, right now. The breathing in of fresh mountain air, the eyes that can see the beauty of the day, the ears that can hear the sweet refrain of birds singing the Alleluia choir to their maker. These are the blessings upon us. The dash between the years upon the gravestone is the story of our days. Those days are the hours that mattered, from boring tasks of laundry and chores, to breakfast in the bowl, and babies to be tended. Those moments are in fact complete and total blessings, but we have taken them for granted. Countless minutes, if we are lucky, to live this life with all of its mundane graces. Those moments are, in fact, unheard of, when related to the child in another part of the world, who lives day after day, sleeping on dirt and foraging for food. That child did nothing but be born in different circumstances of which they have no control. Even in my darkest times, when every food caused me an adverse reaction, I had the option of reaching into a refrigerator in hopes of finding the one food my body would accept, and knowing between the prayer and medicine available to me, my body might rebound. These are all blessings, and I took none of them for granted. Too often I have seen those who have none of those blessings. In their here and now, they just suffer, naked and alone. In my here and now, I still have those who love and pray for me, all the while my brother lies dying and my mother fades away while beautiful babies with distended bellies and haunted eyes need water that won't kill them. We are the stories in the chapters of God's book, the dashes between the years that tell our stories. While one starves, another gorges and grows obese. While one dies, another is born. In the meantime, flowers rise up from cracks in the sidewalk, and blue skies shine above cloudy, dark days. We must choose to embrace our days, for in fact this is our story, and though we might not know the meaning, might not see the tapestry that is being formed, it's our choice to believe in the goodness of our God who gave us this life. Whether we have been given rain or drought, sunshine and blessings, or pain and sorrow, we all live on borrowed time. God is just, and God is righteous. The Lord giveth, and the Lord taketh away, and blessed be the name of the Lord.

Borrowed Time

Time came when we met face to face
Trusting in some holy place
To carry us in amazing grace
We faltered.
The seasons came and we wilted in the here and now.
Wasted, Time/borrowed.
So we throw away the calendar and live today
Thanking God for what we have now
A gentle breeze, a cup of tea, your hand in mine
Summertime.
A child's face, laughter born, a dog's tail, dirt under my
Fingernails.
Borrowed grace in a wrinkled face.
All is now, no time wasted

Chapter seven

The Red Moon

I am pulled from my bed by my husband who directs my eyes to see this moon. I have been hearing of this moon coming, for months now. I'm fumbling for my flip flops and my glasses after an incredibly trying day of puppies eating medicines and painting ceilings and pulling weeds. I'm so exhausted and yet there it is, behind our giant trees, and we move through the dark pathways trying to get a better view. This moon, this red moon that signals the heavens are sending a message. This moon that looks nothing like itself. "God," we say, "what are you doing?" It's so beautiful and it looks like a huge marble hanging in the sky. I have knelt down on the forest floor, straining for a better look through the trees. I think about the heavens and the earth and God's message and *his* mysteries and *his* heart for all of us who are living in a time like this. This bewildering time of blood red moons and tsunamis and other natural disasters. It's the first time in history the Pope is speaking to Congress while there is total unrest in the Middle East. We are living in a confusing time as images are televised of people's heads being cut off in the name of religion. I am wondering with all these world events unraveling all around us, how does this strangeness become the norm? How does all of this play out in the book that God is writing?

The moon is red and I am looking up into the hundred-year-old trees swaying in the fall air. The stars are everywhere and all I can do is praise *him*. All I can do is receive this remarkable gift that transports me from my pain and exhaustion, to glory in the highest. One way or another we will all see this moon. Many parts of the world are witnessing the eclipse of the moon, at the same moment in all its blood red glory.... signaling what? What are you up to God, on this twenty-seventh day of September 2015 in my sheltered forest in America? "What is coming?" I whisper to *his* listening ear. We can never hide from *Him*. *He* is the author and the finisher of this crazy planet. I can only lay on my back and let the stars swallow me up as the trees dance.

~~~

The moon takes its energy from the sun and it reflects it back to the earth. Some nights it sits quietly in a tiny sliver of promise and other nights it leads you by its soft light to the corners of your life. When I was a child and had read a children's book about it being made of cheese, I imagined it to be edible. The science of the moon, that the astronaut John Glenn brought to us as he circled her, brought a new understanding that she was her own planetary destination. At least that was how I viewed her. I began to understand that the moon was more of a symbol of something in our earthly hearts. Longing, grief, mystery, romance. When it was eclipsed by the earth, I learned what no science class had ever taught me. The moon and the sun, dance. They dance and they cast shadows on the earth. Singer Cat Stevens taught me that I was being followed by a moon shadow. I saw it many times growing up. The harvest moon rising across the skies and I, chasing it with reckless abandon, wishing to touch its glory.

The night I was seventeen and in love for the first time, we lay on his parent's roof, held hands and made love by a defining moon. His beard, that he refused to shave, left razor burns upon my chin, which I covered with my mom's make-up, and treasured it as my defining moment of becoming a woman. I wasn't remembering the maker of the moon during that time, though he, raised catholic, and I, raised skid marks to the church, were both feeling like we were guilty of something bad. That first love, and the guilt, bound us in our adolescent journey to find ourselves. Many years later when we parted ways, I thought of him every full moon. So in large measure, the moon defined my growing up, trying to become a woman. It was my own personal history under her shadowed glory.

Now it is defining all of history. The four blood moons have occurred in the past two years, divided by a full solar eclipse in-between. The super, blood-red moon occurs during the first day of the Jewish Feast of the Tabernacles. All four of these moons have occurred on the dates of Jewish feasts. Biblical scholars have long taught that Jesus will return during the Feast of Tabernacles. The only major feast left to fulfill is the Feast of the Tabernacles. Also, if the past is any indication of the future, the blood-red moons represent trouble for Israel.

They reportedly happened during the War of Independence in 1949 and again before the Six Day War in 1967. *

~~~

For now, the moon has all of me, this night in the forest light, with my husband and my thoughts of God. I am bathed in the memories and my breath is caught in my throat, wondering, will I ever not be so small beneath the sky? God's moon is a whimsical love song, gently calling my name. I am waiting patiently for *him* to come and pick me up, and we'll dance by the light of it. Its touch caresses my soul, as *he* directs the Universe and every living thing, defining me as small as my shadow against the forest floor.

Chapter eight

Wanderings

Mother Teresa said, "If we have no peace, it is because we have forgotten we belong to each other." I have long listened to the words of Mother, that tiny package of love in a planet that is lost. She was a voice that carried the weight of her calling. She was not one to shun suffering or horror. Quite the contrary, she called it by name. She tenderly knelt beside a nameless, maggot-infested person, and pulled the disgusting bugs from their dying form. They died knowing they were cared for. They died knowing they were not alone. Mother saw Jesus in everyone. It was how she was able to do her work.

I was a cocky girl with big dreams of stardom and fame when a Colorado newspaper invited me to be interviewed for "People to Watch." The reporter said she was going to ask me, in a rapid fire manner, a set of questions, and she wanted my very first thought to be verbalized. No editing of my answers. She wanted to know the person who sat across from her. I nodded, dressed in my leather skirt, high heels, and fake fingernails, painted red. The questions came; "Favorite car? Favorite food? First job?" etc. etc... I rattled off my answers, and when the question came, "Person you most want to meet?" I said, "Mother Teresa." I was amazed by that, and so was the reporter. It was not in character with the girl in the leather skirt. I was not Catholic (not by a long shot), and I truly knew very little about the nun in Calcutta. It would be years later that she would enter into my life in the strangest of circumstances.

Years of cameras, sound checks, modeling, fast cars and pretty boys. Years of wandering through the auditions, the tours, the nightclubs and the bands. Years of finding Jesus on my deathbed, going into the lighted tunnel, hearing *his* voice, and walking through fire. There were refining fires of all shapes and sizes. A changing of the guards in my heart. The transfusion of *his* blood with mine bringing peace to my twisted wreckage of a life. Miracles, scourging, tenderness, rejection, and pain. Daily pain, without measure. I lashed at God on more than one occasion. Never a church lady, I was always pushing the boundaries of propriety.

While tithing on Colfax Ave in Denver, I would be led down darkened alleyways to dumpsters, where a broken man or woman lay. "God sent me," I would say. We would weep together, mingling tears; those broken addicts, with no teeth, and me. We were a beautiful sight, in retrospect. Leaning into the grace that only God can do. I was soothed in my faith until something unexpected would come and I would fail the test of staying in *his* peace over and over again.

Sharing a bed without a wedding ring. Cussing out loud, wanting my own way, and not trusting God. The church judged me. Shunned and left out to dry, I understood I was not doing it well, this "church" thing, yet doing it I did. Prison ministry, street ministry; people were saved, and people sensing God through this broken vessel called Lynn. He moved through me in spite of me. Grace.

~~~

Walking in the maximum security prison into death row, I am with a guard. Heavy doors of steel have shut over and over. My hands are clammy; my heart is pounding. I am praying, quietly sensing the pulse of evil in the walls, hearing the cries of the broken souls silently screaming from behind closed doors. I can only see their eyes as we walk past...they begin to call out curses, slithering tongues come out of the narrow slits in the doors. They start to freak out, a whole row of them, as I walk past.

The guard was stunned... "I've never seen anything like that," he said.

I began to pray for them, and the scripture about the demon calling out to Jesus, "What do you want with us, Jesus of Nazareth?" came to mind. I am far from being perfect as Christ is, but I was carrying *him* with me that day in spirit and in anointing. The demons saw Christ in me and all hell broke loose. It was humbling.

I was trying to become the next prison chaplain, as the long standing chaplain was moving to an inner-city church in Denver. I was there almost a year, waiting for their verdict on me.

I finally moved back to Denver and purchased a condo in the city. The very day I moved in, the prison offered me the job. I was not going back, and I felt no peace about going back but I felt adrift.

I wandered some more, trying to find *his* will. I was in a large church every time the door was open. I was sick in body and desperate for *his* touch. My wandering heart found another relationship out of *his* will. After three years and another near death miracle in ICU, I turned forty years old. I left the relationship out of obedience to God, praying *he* would bring him back to me. He did not come back and one year later I said "I do" to my cowboy.

~~~

We can wander and be completely lost, and God will redeem us. After nearly twenty years together, my cowboy and I know all about wandering and feeling forsaken, and we know about grace. We have survived our broken marriage over and over again. The miracle is, we love each other deeply, cracked pots, twisted wreckage, and all. Beauty for ashes you might say. He is a gift, and I am thankful. We are the mirror of God's grace one to another.

~~~

I am struggling in the season of Lent. Struggling with hate, in the name of religion. Struggling with judgment, above grace. Struggling with the battle lines, the "my way or the highway" rigidity. This right and that right and "they shouldn't have rights" and "they need to change" and do it this way or believe that way. All I see about Jesus is, *he* loves them. The broken, the harlots, the tax collectors, the criminals, the lost, the downtrodden, and the sick. *He* never once mentions homosexuality in *his* ministry. *He* never once mentions the babies left on the side of the road in *his* time, unwanted. **Jesus is not political, *he* is spiritual**. *He* sees the need and *he* answers it with love. So after sitting in the pew and sensing the deep love shared all around us, as we break bread and sing hymns, and those of us gathered together hear the cracked bell of redemption that rings over the town square, bathing us in the peace that "surpasses all understanding"; why do I hear two of the church gossiping and slandering another? It's like a poisonous mist shutting out the grace, which had covered us like a warm blanket. Mocking the Holy of Holy, the Christ. That beautiful grace which we mock every time we fight and squabble and play judge and jury. Placing judgment above love, and hate above mercy. Judgment slams the door to God's presence. It's what keeps many of us from finding his love through the church.

~~~

    I am wandering in a local shop in a daze of pain. Losses have mounted and my heart is empty. I am the vacant, I am on the bone weary sojourn of the cross bearer. Lost in thought and not fully present, I see a book sitting there, entitled "Works of Love Are Works of Peace" by a man named Michael Collopy. I pick the book up and it is a book on Mother Teresa. I scan the photos and then put it down. I walked away to another part of the store and felt drawn back to the book. I picked it up again and began to read a bit of it and when I saw the price I put it back down. Much like a homing pigeon I return to the book. Finally, carrying it closely to my heart, I take it up and I pay for it. More money than I have to throw away. How it will fast become priceless to me.

    I go home and climb into my claw foot bath tub and read the afternoon away. By the time I have read the book I am in tears. I feel the same pull, as I had felt this morning to pick up the book, only this time, I am to contact the author, Michael Collopy. I have never heard of this man before. I Google him and found his email for a project he has for peace makers. I write to him and thank him for writing such a moving book. How it inspired me to keep going, how it brought God's tangible hand to me when I needed it most. In the email, I include a link to my music website and I go to bed.

The next morning, I get an email from Michael. He thanked me for the encouraging words. He thanked me for taking the time to write to him, and he had listened to my songs. Could he please call me? I send him my phone number and the very next day, while sitting in a public bathroom, my phone rings. A male voice asked me if this was Lynn Schriner.

"Yes."

"This is Michael Collopy."

He asks if it was a bad time. I am saying no. We talk for hours that morning. Mostly about Mother Teresa: her heart, her thoughts, her life. He had spent almost fifteen years with her, and before she passed away to go be with her Lord, she turned to Michael and told him that she had a talk with God, and she asked the Lord for a favor of sorts. She knew there would be people who would come after her that would need her help, and could the Lord allow her to help them? She felt God had said yes; she felt a lot of peace about that. I am hanging on his every word.

"I believe that you are one of those people," Michael says. "I believe she is watching over you and helping you, and I want to send you something from her."

I am overwhelmed with joy and disbelief. I am rolling in the deep, finding myself at a loss. Surely this is a joke. Mother Teresa, Noble Peace Prize winner, and humanitarian. Me, in my Volkswagen beetle, barely able to function most days, helping a few orphans in Africa. Mother Teresa, *my* guardian? Michael then says that he wants to bring me out to San Francisco and meet Quincy Jones, perhaps do a concert. He wants to introduce me to Matt Damon who was doing water projects as well. There are moments of time where the questions become larger than the gift.

I hear myself say to Michael, "I would so love that, but I am sick. I can't travel and it's not the right time."

I hear Michael respond, "I am so sorry to hear this. I will be praying for you. We'll see what God's going to do."

I thank him through my tears. I hear his gentle words of encouragement and love. I drive home and the brakes fail in the VW. Trying to turn a corner and the brake pedal goes to the floor.

I manage to get the car home. I manage to share the story of Mother Teresa with my husband. I feel defeated because of my sickness. I feel condemnation from my lack of faith to step out, fly to San Francisco, and meet Michael and Quincy and Matt. For a moment I almost called Michael back, to tell him I was coming. Instead, I crawl into bed and cry my eyes out. A week later a package comes. Inside was a rosary.

It's been two and half years since that conversation with Michael. He has gone off photographing the Dali Lama. I have been fighting for my life after the poisons came. I sense that GOD is not through with me yet. I sense that one day I will pick up a phone and speak with Michael and fly on a plane. One fine day, the wandering and the wondering will become a certainty, and I will go. In the meantime, I pick up her rosary and I touch it to my heart and to my lips and wonder at the gift. Believing that her beautiful prayers are covering me, just as she believed before she passed.

In the Third Watch of the Night

Under a star-crossed sky
I seek your face,
Under a soft blanket of grace.
I know you are there
Though I can't quite catch your scent in the air.
I am, after all, only your child
You're the keeper of me
Tears and all,
Fears and falling down.
You are the keeper of me
Fraught and frail,
You are my anchor in a deep storm
The keeper of me.
I listen to lies that threaten to make a liar out of my faith
I know that under the heavens
I am on my knees,
And across the world
As it shakes and roars,
United by love,
We are, after all, only your children....
Wandering across the galaxy of hope,

The Keeper of Me

We hang on your every word,

Longing to fit our tiny faith into your hand of grace.

Though we may doubt with whispers,

By which we wander and wonder where you are,

We are tiny in our wisdom

Amongst your brilliant stars.

After all we are only your collective children

And

You the Keeper

Chapter nine

Lone Thoughts from a High Wire

Why have I come to this place, this planet, this time in history? I am a wandering woman, a vagabond of the desires that we commonly share. I am a fierce warrior and a flame, in *his* directive. I have forgotten the messages and the sweet whispers of tenderness in the fight. One long at war loses the attribute of kindness in the battle for survival. Why have I come, Lord? Have I only come to witness this moment, this gateway to heaven, this hell on earth? With your grace, and the tears of healing balm covering the carnage, will the sharing and breaking of bread, the shedding of the blood, bring the peace I seek? It's for your glory, of that I am clear. I am kneeling on the earth, and I know Jesus walked on water, but I can't seem to gather the courage to step out of the boat. Why have I come? I am a wife and a friend, a teacher and a muse. I am your child, Father, living to see your beautiful face and carry *your* love, but it seems I am carrying your cross too. My soul cries out "What do you want? I don't want to break your heart Lord." Not with my words or my thoughts or my heart, encased with desires that are not of your own. I am full of revelation without exhalation. I am hearing and sensing the kingdom of your glory, like a divine gem of truth on the streets of gold, and like the washing of the feet and the breaking of the bread, I want this connection with you so much. I want it to be something greater than the ritual of the sacrifice. I want it to be filled with your language Lord, the language of love. I want to be full enough to spill over everywhere I go. I want to see your face in everything and everyone. The heart knows its reflection. Help me to behold the mystery.

~~~

The moon has been pulling me in the night to notice the play of its light against my upturned face in the open window. I am returning to dreams, though the mind is chattering like many birds on a wire, chattering birds of thoughts and worries, stealing my peace. If I listen carefully, a lone bird is speaking softly, "Peace be still."

Not anxious or afraid, but trusting that God is in control and will make all things right, in *his* time. I must listen hard to hear the lone bird's voice, which is easily drowned out by the roar of chattering birds on the wire above.

    Let me stop and breathe, and say a prayer for peace. Let me have ears to hear and eyes to see the better way. The way of peace. The moon is rising and the pull is great. God is sitting as *he* will, in the light reflecting my soul. *He* is always there, as *he* is everywhere. *He* is the lone voice, *he* is the gentle breeze, *he* is the babies' cry, and *he* is the mirror for me. "Oh Lord, be *thou* my vision. You are ever before me." I rest, content.

Life is Only a Reflection

The moon catches the field bunny as she scurries to safety in the barn. An owl watches her from the top of the pole but does not desire to partake of her. She will live to see another day.

Life is only a reflection.

A tiny moon dances between the bunny and the owl. Nothing wasted, nothing needed. They do not needlessly kill, these animals of truth. They are not like us. We lash at our reflections, see less than joy in our hearts, and blame one another. We eat without hunger and grow sick. We weaken when we compare ourselves to another, as if we hold up a mirror to another's faults and failings, while we cloak our own under the dark of night. We are only a reflection of the truth.

Life is only a reflection.
When God enters into us and we reflect *his* love, the world opens with arms that splay joy, smiles brightly, and

treads tenderly upon the earth. We give, and do not squander any piece of the joy, wrapped in *his* glory. The spirit of ecstasy will carry us. Life is only a reflection of that which we carry within. So let us not hold a bright light to the wounds, let us not expose one another to shame. Let us only shelter one another in the midst of our deepest pain.

When I see that which disgusts me in you, that which I carry within me, like a wild untamed shadow, waiting for the right directive of circumstance to implode the underbelly of our scarred truth, I see that we are the same, you and I.

Life is only a reflection.

In our truth waiting to be revealed, you will turn your hand up to mine and I will lay it gently down and the moon will capture our eyes. Truth revealed, time heals, and skin to skin we reflect upon upturned hearts and roads less traveled…and see our reflections.

Chapter ten

Earth is a School

the lesson

The earth is a school, a divine process by which we are each given our own unique set of shoes to walk in it. We are given a divine road map, a whisper from our loving *father* who ordained and stamped each one of us with *his* holy stamp.

He marks our path, and much like glowing beacons of light, we begin our journey to find our purpose on this earth. We all have one, specifically made in *his* image, to be *his* hands and feet, *his* heart and mind, to reach out to a hurting world. *His* volume is turned so low in the chaos of noise—called planet earth—that if we are not careful, we will miss *his* still, small voice that will not shout above the noise. Yet, when we listen, we shine brightly with *his* spirit. We are not an accident, nor are we a mistake. No matter what has been said about you, you are here because God willed it so. We were created with longing in us, *his* created beings, to be with *him*. To search the skies, the seas, the hearts of other created beings, to see *his* face, and to hear *his* voice. God resides in every created being as surely as the mysterious laminin which *he* has placed inside every cell of our bodies. This divine glue holds us together and is shaped perfectly in the image of a cross, which I believe our Savior's death stamped on every cell in our bodies, *his* holy seal of love and life. No, we are not here by mistake. We are here because God, the perfect love, the divine Creator of heaven and earth, has created us, called us by name, and placed us here in our classroom. We will learn, mostly through pain, grief, loss and love, that God has a destiny for you and for me. *He* is after all no respecter of persons, meaning that what *he* has done for the least of these, *he* has also done for us. Believe that *he* loves you and you have *his* love.

    You have *his* love to carry you through the darkest of nights and to extend into the darkness; *his* light, by which others can see. Love changes us, teaches us, corrects us, and yes, allows us to experience deep and darkened times that shred our faith, and then gently rebuilds us once again. Love is not the slick, sexy message that the world gives. Love is in form and light that carries us through losses so staggering we stumble, fall, and feel forsaken. We will know not the love until *he* stirs within us the ability to believe again. Believe that all is not lost, believe that what is shredding every fiber of our beings will be used for love—if we let it.

God tests us and brings *his* grace in the most painful of places, and lets us go for a while to walk in shoes that do not yet fit us. Like a small child under the watchful eye of a loving father, we take tentative and stumbling steps into water that is rising. The river runs high, and just when we despair for our very lives, *he* says *"Believe"* and calms the fearful, beating heart, then sets our feet to dare to walk on water, as Peter did, following after Christ. *"Believe!"* cries out our Christ, the Savior. *"Believe and receive, love your enemies, be my hands and feet. Touch me,"* God says. And *"Yea though you walk through the valley of the shadow of death I will be with you. I will never fail nor forsake you."*

So suffering does not mean forsaken, rejection does not mean forsaken, sickness and even death do not mean forsaken. No, contrary to that, God loves us so much that suffering comes, and in that suffering, *he* invites us to believe. Believe against all feelings to the contrary, that *he* loves us. Loves us so deeply that *he* sent the homeless and forsaken Savior, Jesus Christ, *his* son, the Holy One. The divine love of all love. The risen Lord who dared those who doubted *his* love to touch *his* nail scarred hands who came to be with us. And in *his* suffering sacrifice, all we must do is believe in that love. Believe.

Believe that we who stumble and screw up and lose heart and faith, who won't forgive one another, who fight and mourn and gossip and slander and roll in the deep, are still capable of receiving *his* love in spite of ourselves. Which brings us to the highest lesson in this classroom called life: Love, in GOD form. God's love is a love that is wild and without boundaries. Crazy love that never cries out, "You owe me." Love that covers you when you are less than your divine self and purpose. A love that believes in the goodness of others and not their mistakes. Love that walks without knowing where love is leading. It just trusts that love always takes us through the darkness and shares the truth of this intimate, holy, divine love that leans in closely and whispers our destiny in our ear.

Your hardest times often lead to the greatest moments of your life.
Keep the faith.
It will all be worth it in the end.

Chapter eleven

Messengers

Messengers, feathered and sweet. I am a young girl locked in a room that is my prison, on oxygen. The world and its poisons have become my jailer. I am in pain and unable to eat, sleep, or breathe in any kind of normal fashion. I am skin and bones, hiding in a room, longing for a normal day. My mom and I are constantly at odds as she continues to smoke cigarettes in the house. Dad is working, long hours of work. They slide in and out of the room I am in for brief moments. The only other visitors to my room are my cousin Darcy, who came that summer and hung out with me, and a neighbor boy named Gus. Most times it was just God and me and the briefest touch from a parent. I am lonely and obsessed with the idea that I have no hope. I am twenty years of age and growing old, with my untamed hair, and night gowns with stains on them. I have grown "allergic" to the world after a pesticide poisoning in a city park. My body, once a gymnast who competed against Cathy Rigby, a gold medalist, once a downhill skier who kept right on the tail of Olympic skier Billy Kidd, in the downhill course of Steamboat Springs, and climbed Mount Poppa in Mexico with a forty-pound pack on my back, this body that was once so strong, I won every blue ribbon in the all-school field day, is broken. The body that ate every food under the sun, is now unable to digest any food at all. I am living on something that the doctor prescribed. A sixty dollar-a-box powder that sustained the astronauts, made of sugar, vitamins, and calories. It tastes like raw potatoes. I am so broken that the doctors sent me home to die.

Amidst the pain, the isolation, the malnutrition, and the hunger, I am hungry for life, and I am beating back death. I am sitting in the room on oxygen, looking out the window and crying out to God, "Please, I need a sign that you are still with me!" as tears stream down my face.

"Please God, I feel so forsaken!" The words have left my lips and I rub my eyes to focus, when I see her. She is tiny and yellow and flitting above the back yard and into the large oak tree. I am straining to watch her fly when suddenly she flies straight up to the window where I am sitting and she just looks at me. My breath catches in my throat and I am completely unaware of time, the pain suspended in this moment—God has sent the messenger. I am holding my breath as she watches me for another moment, and then she is gone. I release my breath and praise God. The next day she comes again, and the next, and the next. For three days she comes, flying in her usual pattern and then straight up to me in the window. It is my first flight into a realm of God's dominion over *his* created beings. The Bible says that even the rocks will cry out if the people won't praise. I am praising God, and I am covered in *his* grace and a tiny winged angel is bringing me his message. "I have not forgotten you."

   The messenger of the finch at my window was one as powerful as that of the rainbow to Noah. For over forty years at various times of heartache and struggle, the finch has come to me. Sometimes in bunches, sometimes alone. They are always yellow, and they always land or fly right in front of me. I am, at those moments, still the child in the window. Where no human voice or touch can be found, God sends me *his* creatures. Beautiful winged and furry messengers of love.

In the past two years I have lost my brother, my mother, and my beloved dog, Layla. I have lost friends to death and indifference. I have lost a home and my already fragile health. I have been shown, in my weakened state, my need of profound refining. I have come close to the edge of me, that place where the wild things are. Emotions become super-sized under the magnification of loss and pain. I have done the dance of faith, time and time again, forcing my heart to look toward God and *his* promises. There has been little to sustain me in the realm of reality, but that is the measure of faith by its very definition. Faith is the substance of things not seen, the substance of things hoped for. Believing in God's goodness when all is well, is easy. Believing in God's goodness in the middle of a storm, takes faith. I stagger with the load, and when well-meaning people, that are blessed, say "Give it to Jesus," my response inside isn't very Christian. I am in a place of bewilderment, wandering in the wilderness both literally and metaphorically. All I know to do is to share this journey of suffering with others so that twilight lifts for a moment. I am learning that to feel crazy at times is very normal under extreme stress. Pain brings anger. The facts are that when I am running as fast as I can and my circumstances are out of control, and then people judge me and are angry or indifferent because they have no concept by which to understand my journey, I want to escape. To race ahead of the pain and see into a beautiful future. God in *his* amazing wisdom says to *"Be still and know that I am God."* I am to rest in the moments of pain that go on and on. Wisdom says to live, now, in this fractured moment. To let the pain rise inside me, to bow down on the country road that I am living on, and seek *his* face.

There are mourning doves cooing from their perch on the fence in front of me in my moment of throwing myself at God's feet. I am reminded how often God used doves to bring a message to *his* people. Peace and the Holy Spirit. A branch in the aftermath of a flood.

I am praying for his peace in a dry and barren land, as antelope watch from a distance, the cries of my suffering.

~~~

A Thousand Soaring Birds

A thousand soaring birds of flight

The Keeper of Me

Coming into the field at early light
Their wings are illuminated as they come
A thousand upon the frozen ground.

They bring in every sway of dance
The truth of a creator who calls them home
Amidst the noise of city dwellings
Cars and horns and indifferent fellows.

I see their strength in numbers of love
Following one another in patterns of arrows
Pointing their way toward home.
And when one wearies, and grows tired of the journey
Falling back,
Another will come and support the effort.
Together they carry on to the next earthly night
Resting side by side
In fields under the stars
In sleeping sight.

They awaken before dawn and carry their hearts
Another day together

Charting their course.
A thousand upon the frozen ground

Rising ever onward.
A thousand soaring birds
In early light
No squabbling, not a fight
They know their purpose
They carry their dreams
A thousand soaring birds.

They crown the earth,
Their wings are singing,
It is their meaning.

Life is a series of a thousand tiny miracles.

Notice them

Chapter twelve

Feast of Miracles

"Oh feast your eyes on the miracles of life." I say though no one is listening, and a yellow and black monarch butterfly floats by in the morning breeze and alights like a fairy on a yellow sunflower, whose face is tipped upward into the dawn's early light. I stretch hard and move high my fingers to touch the dawn. The birds cock their heads when I coo, and they seem to fluff up a little bigger. It is then that I hear the praise of all praises coming from somewhere behind me in the field. The Celine Dion of the bird world has joined the choir and is giving voice to its maker. There are miracles all around me as the sun peeks through to welcome another day on planet earth. In a world full of lies and pain there is promise. This holy, divine wake-up call bringing *his* son to our darkness. After a hot, pain wracked night, I know light will rise and chase away my lonely fears. The midnight shadows and wild unimaginable dangers that left me trembling in my pain, is now evaporating into the miracle of the sunrise. I can shake the night off as easily as the robins shake the water off their backs in the stream. A wise man awakens every day to a new life. Fullness of joy comes when, along with the berries in my cereal, I fill up on *his* grace. Grace is food for the wretched sinner that I know myself to be. The miracle of grace is that *he* sends this dawn, and the birds, and the light, and as I feast on *his* miracles, I can ask *him* to give me *his* eyes that I will not miss one gift *he* wishes to give. I can call out "Here I am Lord" in the garden of grace and we will meet face to Holy face. *His* reflection shining so brightly that if I linger, I will burn. If I can stand to be so close to God, the miracle of love will reveal to me all my imperfections, washed clean in *His* light. The feast of miracles, the beauty and the strength, the promises and the truth, have taken my breath, and humbles me gently. I don't feel guilt or shame, but I am naked in *his* love. To become another miracle of the day by smiling or gently assisting another weary miracle. For indeed we all are. Miracles are being grace to one another, forgiveness, and light in the darkness. "May all who see me, see you" is my daily bread, as I drink deeply of the cup of God soup. God is generous and God is good and *he* wants to fill *his* children up. From Africa to India to America, we cry our lonely cry for God to fill us. I have seen God answer the cries of another through me. I have seen African babies receive God in the drilling of water wells and being fed a vitamin enriched gruel that is much like manna from heaven to them. Those precious children are thankful and they will live.

I treasure the blue bonnets that scatter seeds along the ground as the doves come and find food and drink. Doves are divine creatures of flight, and some things we share in common, like committing ourselves in a form of matrimony, till death do us part. I marvel that they never seem to squabble over the seed that I have left. One will stand watch while another bathes, one will fly and the other will follow quietly without complaint. So much of God's feast involves teachers without language. They teach by living out their innate God presence and directive within their tiny beating hearts. They worry not, and they care only about what is before them. They tend and work and fluff and build and drink from the stream and sleep amongst the branches of shelter and safety.

There has been a teacher in my life with soft brown eyes and a long fluffy tail, who watched my every move and strived with all of her being to please me. She forgave any slight of the human kind, such as leaving her too long alone. She trusted that I would provide, protect and love her, and I did. With all my heart, as she gave me all of hers. She worshiped and adored me. She taught me in her humble ways so much about God and *his* unconditional love. I see God in animals more than I do in most people. She sat with me while I was sick or in pain, watched over me when she sensed weakness, rejoiced with me as we walked through a lifetime of sunny mornings, and huddled with me in the storms. She traveled beside me in cars, calm and confident, never telling me which way to go. She trusted me to do what was best for her. Interesting that dog is God backwards. I wonder if Adam knew how much like God, dogs seem to be, when he named them. She was a great gift and sixteen years of love taught me much. She lays now in our forest under a plaque, "Beloved."

~~~

Oh Divine, Holy God, who led the Jews into the

wilderness and parted the Red Sea, turned water into wine, healed the deaf, the leper and the blind, you are so divine, so holy, so unreachable and unattainable and yet, you are so near, so warm and so close. I sometimes feel your breath on my cheek. Why must I question you? Why can't I be more like my beloved dog who taught me so much about you? The greatest feast of miracles will come when I can stop questioning, stop searching to understand, and just jump straight into your arms. Accepting that which I will never fully understand. I am finite and you are infinite. Help me sweet keeper of me, to accept by faith, your hand upon my furrowed brow, your presence behind me and before me, your silent pressing on my heart, and your gentle correction in my spirit. By faith I receive and accept your many blessings; breath, sleep, food and love. Birds fly, gravity holds us here, the sun rises and sets, the earth turns on its axis. Faith without question occurs with these things. Why is it so hard to let go?

"The Lord giveth and the Lord taketh away and blessed be the name of the Lord." If I could rewind my life, I would see all of the millions of moments of confusion and pain and just know you were there. Always with me, never leaving me. As your child, let me believe without measure your love upon my life. Your living water which turns a parched and weary desert into an ocean blue in a forest of green. You have all of us at the banquet table, setting our places as you did with your disciples, feeding us the nourishment that never ceases. Help me to not backward gaze, but to lay my forehead against yours God, and sense your smile. Help me to lean against you as John did at the last supper and relax in your presence.

~~~

Gardens & Grace

I love a garden. Life pushes through the hard soil after a freezing winter, and lights up the spring with their little hopeful shoots of glee, straining for the light and the warmth. They inspire me, those shoots, they challenge me to care about them and to nurture their efforts. In nurturing them they nurture me. It's this amazing dance of life. When that little shoot becomes a flower, that has overcome so much to bring its beauty and its purpose to the garden, it will nourish the birds and the bees, and stun us with the visual color and light that is painted by the hand of its creator, and mine. I am in awe of its beauty. I will bury my face in its fragrance and marvel at the grace by which God grows *his* garden. I ask to be a metaphor of this grace.

All new life comes from darkened places. That which is planted deeply will one day come forth into the light. Like a seed in the earth, like a baby in a womb. Like a word from a writer's heart.

~~~

The Keeper of Me / 91

The sky has swept the day away
And painted stars of depth and center
The middle of the night is caressing the moon and I feel small. I look up, the sky is suddenly upon me and I am swept away into star struck wonder. The universe goes silent inside my head. Starry, starry night. Amen

Chapter thirteen

Mission of Joy

One morning in late October, I go searching. I have a pocketful of money and I am seeking souls to feed. The chill of the morning and the ache of my body are an indication of my hearts condition. Whenever I start to feel my heart grow cold I go in search of another's need. There is a street called "the longest street in America", and on that street live the many faces of despair. There is the stench of urine, and scattered everywhere, are bottles of oblivion and needles of pain. I see faces huddled around alleyways and cloaked in darkened doorways. They are sitting and talking and fighting and sharing their "fix". I'm driving my old Jeep, praying and asking Christ which ones are ready for *his* touch. I see an older woman in a threadbare coat with a cigarette hanging from her lips. I sense a gentle prodding *"Stop." so* I pull the Jeep over to the curb and step out. She eyes me with suspicion as I walk towards her. "Hello, how are you today?" I ask. She drops her eyes and fumbles in her torn pocket for a lighter avoiding my eyes. "I was led today to come to you and tell you that Jesus loves you." She looks up and her eyes soften. She drops the cigarette and fumbles again in that tattered coat she wears, and in her gnarled hand she pulls out a small worn bible. We smile at one another with such love that I feel overcome and touch her cheek. As we draw near to one another I slip a fifty-dollar bill into her pocket. The hug is warm. Our breath is close and I see her smile a big toothless grin at me. Not a word has been exchanged by her so I wave and walk away.

"Thank you!" I hear her say. She means thank you for the message because she has yet to find the money in her pocket. I feel full, knowing she will find it shortly and I pray she will not use it for anything but food.

"*That is not your business*" I hear the spirit of love say to me gently. So I climb back into my Jeep and move on. I see person after person, there is so much need, and I keep straining to sense the gentle prodding as to whom *He* would have me stop for. Sensing nothing, I am about to stop and try again later when I know intuitively to turn down into an alleyway. I park the Jeep and get out. I am surprisingly unafraid, a solitary woman in a darkened alleyway on a street that is notorious for violence. I see no one but I am being led gently by the spirit towards a large dumpster at the very end of the alley. "*There.*" the gentle prodding again. I edge my way up to the dumpster and looking down I see a man curled on his side as if asleep. I can smell him; it has been long since he had a proper bath. I have startled him and he looks up at me in a panic with eyes that are red and blood shot.

"Hello" I say gently and he replies

"Hello." in a shy, booze soaked voice.

"I'm here for you because God sent me here." He looks frightened and I continue softly, "You are not forgotten." Those words are not mine own, I know that. They are words of grace and mercy and love from the Father that knows *his* child. I kneel down beside him and reach my hand out. "He sent me today to tell you that you are not forgotten, that *he* loves you and *he* hears your cries." My hand touches his filthy coat and when I touch him, he begins to weep.

"*He* said that? *He* hears me?" I nod and see the shattered dreams of this broken man in the full light of God's glory.

The cry from his thorny heart, broken in an alleyway and living amongst the trash, because he feels that he is trash, is illuminated in the bright glory of God. There is nothing but naked truth between us and that truth is love. "For God so loved the world that he gave his only begotten son that whosoever shall believe in him shall not perish but have ever lasting life."

I have felt this man's pain of self-loathing, tasted the bitter truth of all the masks pulled back and raw truth revealed. He stands up beside me, swaying slightly, and we put our arms around each other, one to the other. I break into a trembling and there are fireworks of joy raining down from the heavens upon us. One smelly, homeless man in an alley and one small, broken girl in a Jeep; both the apple of their Father's eye. I drop my hand into my pocket and pull out the remaining wad of money.

"Here is another gift from the Father to you. *He* loves you so much!" I am weeping now, my tears dropping onto his hand. "*He* loves you so much." I turn to go and he gently kisses my cheek. He is no longer the lost and broken man drunk in the alleyway. He is suddenly the lips of Christ and he is tenderly kissing my cheek.

"God bless you!" he says, his eyes alive with love.

We part in a deep and abiding current of love. I found joy in search of blessing another. I found a brother lying in the cover of darkness. God saw *his* beloved child alone and cold and hearing his cries, *he* sent me, a broken version of angelic, to be *his* hands and feet. In obedience, two of *his* kids are grace to one another. Is love truly as simple as that? *His* message of grace is pure, and singing loudly in my soul as I drive slowly home, forever changed. We are all tattered angels.

Chapter fourteen

Touchstone

I have searched long for God. I learned young that I was very broken. Broken in a way that left me wide open. For takers, and con-artists of the emotional kind. I was a target, a bright flashing light of pain. The heavens and the devil have wrestled hard for me. I often make the devil dance, and still, God has me close. I am thankful I don't have to be perfect to be loved. God doesn't need my perfection. The need for perfection is the mirage of a failed species called mankind. They are wearing the armor of illusions to protect them from themselves. Denial is a powerful thing. It keeps the blinders on those behaviors and feelings that allow the broken things to become acceptable. It's comfortable to live in denial because it requires little accountability. We live there until we can't. We live there until we are forced to recognize our helplessness. Some of us learn that we are wounded and broken early on. Some of us are smacked down later. We will all face our brokenness. We will all face ourselves one day and know that we contributed to another's pain. We will all have to say that we didn't always do our best. That we took the broad road instead of the narrow gate. That we lied, stole, cheated, judged and criticized, and were indifferent to another's suffering. That we ignored a need. We withheld love, money, clothing and food from the least of these. That orphans died so we could buy our designer shoes or go on vacations because we would not share. It's not been a conscious choice typically, it just comes from an indifference and an entitlement that says we are more important. That our needs are more important. That we deserve our money, after all, we worked for it. A child in Africa can't work. They have no shoes on their feet, nor can they expect their government to care for their needs. Welfare doesn't exist in Africa like it does in America. They cry out to anyone who will have ears to hear them. If we can't hear them, it's because we are not listening. God, my touchstone, gave me ears to hear the African cries. He also carries me to lost men and women on the streets in America and to the Native Americans, who are trapped in poverty right here in the U.S. If we care enough to hear these cries and we do something, anything about it, a burden, a suffering, could be and would be, lifted. It's not that hard really. Give up a Starbucks once a week and put the money in a jar. Our flavored coffee costs would feed a child in a third world country for a month.

~~~

A touchstone is how we gauge the value of a thing...it's the measure by which I come to God for my answers. I live in the land of wanting. I want to be of service to my fellow man and I want to find the touch of God in the mundane of my days upon my sick bed. I want to understand, but it doesn't change a thing even when I do. This trip around the sun has an expiration date and one-day mine will be up. I want a lot of time to make my life matter, but what if it matters not? I have already outlived the prognosis, from so many doctors, for the length of my days. I want every second to count for something valuable, or what's the point of the suffering? I live intensely aware of the cost for everything and I'm sure, to a healthy person, I might appear neurotic and hyper vigilant. I don't take much for granted and I don't miss much. I can't easily let down and relax. I know I am not a human "doing", but I feel empty of energy if I am not trying. God meanwhile just keeps telling me to rest in *his* arms. "But there are babies out there who need fresh water and food!" I cry out to God, and squirm, exhausted in *his* arms. "The neighbors are hurting and the dog next door barks all day and the house is dirty and cluttered and we don't have enough money!" God just holds me as I continue to fight the inactivity. I am judging God because of my lack. God just waits quietly, and in my angst, the devil watches and dances.

I want to touch God with my faith. I want to see *his* face and yet I see *him* more in my rear view mirror. There is the hind sight to really see *his* presence in every situation. Even the ones where there appears to be no victory at the time. I can't understand my responses sometimes from within my pain. If I can just stay focused on Jesus, I respond better in pain. Why is that so hard? Its dawn's early light, and I am bruised with pain. There is a moment before my eyes open where I seek God behind my lashes and my dreams. I remember the neighbor down the lane whose cat is dying. I say a prayer. I envision my dad in his pajamas, sleeping without my mom beside him. I feel his pain for a moment and I pray. My stomach growls and I know thirst and I remember my beloved orphans and I pray. My man is meeting with the VA clinic today and his pain becomes my silent prayer for healing. My sister/friend is thought of and God is thanked. There are so many needs. Have I missed one? Does it matter? Doesn't God know the silent needs? Doesn't God know the hearts of those who cry out to him before a sound is uttered? It is written, it is sung, and it is wept into existence. Our prayers lay heavy in the dust that floats its way into the light of Gods heart. Our longing for his answers to our needs are carved into our DNA. God is the only answer. I stretch and look out into the forest trees shadowed against the sky that is becoming day. It will be fully present shortly. Much like the answer to our prayers. God is the touchstone of our souls and the maker of our days and there is nothing to do but wait on *his* dawn. So I will wait. *His* answers aren't always as I hope. *His* answers aren't always my heart's desire. I can only see the back side of the tapestry. *His* hands are busy and just because I can't see it, doesn't mean *he* doesn't care. Touch and see the hands that are scarred by the nails. "Oh help my unbelief!" cries out the apostles and me.

Touchstone

I bow my head

I look up

I cry out

I shout

I sigh

I question

I release, I search for peace.

The sky is forever blue

Full of the sounds of longing, winging their way to you

How many cries do you hear upon your wind?

How many Alleluia's are swirling by?

We run across sand and desert and sea

Searching and calling out for you

This touchstone upon the cliff

Tucked under a rock

In a lover's kiss

Snow falls gently

And mist rises

And babies cry

And the lost lift fists

And fire guns

And wail and wail.

Calm or restless you see it all

This night

This day

Nothing and no one is greater than you are.

Nothing and no one brings all of life into your bosom

You are the rock

The touchstone for all of humanity

For all time

Never changing

Scarred perfection at the infliction of your own design

That you might become like us

You died to be our shelter

The touchstone for life

Infinity

Forever

Amen

Chapter fifteen

Amazing Grace

I wake to autumn light. I wake to a train whistle as it comes slowly through the village we call home. I hear the sounds of the forest creatures. I am listening to the leaves dancing, and the trees swaying gently in the breeze. The puppies are tugging a sock, loudly, as they race by. That beautiful man who shares my life is brewing his morning Chai. I sense my stomach growling and I look at the world God has given me, and I am blessed. I want to sit here and gaze long at the blessing of the simple things. God has brought the new day, and if I am not careful, I will miss the gift. I can learn today to give kindness and to live with an open hand. I can learn today how to go deeper into the voice of God and hear *his* very heartbeat. I can learn to rest in *his* arms by leaning in. The table is set for me every morning. If I don't go rushing into the day, *He* will wash my feet, cover me with *his* smile, let me lean in, and *he* will feed me.

Miracles come in the everyday, tiny miracles of grace. Delicate winged creatures, so small, washing their wings. Having just hours to live their lives, they will fly and know their purpose. Lumbering miracles of the brown bear on the mountain searching for the last dinner of choke berries and bird seed, set out for the migrating songbirds. He must find enough fuel to lay him down in slumber for a long winter's nap. Miracles of a marriage that lasts through fires that burn. Miracles of diseases that take out so many lives and yet, leave me here. Miracles of water to wine, artists that paint, songbirds that sing. I am thankful that the sun has risen. I am thankful that the day has begun. I can share this moment and that too is a miracle. An awareness to the hungry soul. There are miracles all around. Those we see and those we miss, our eyes cloudy with the cataracts of our self-desire. "What about me?" cries the inward gazing soul.

~~~

In the cycle of days upon this earth, God raises the sun and settles the moon. *He* paints the sky and *he* covers the ground, and the earth knows *his* touch and the created who live upon *his* canvas miss *his* gifts, and grabble for *his* glory.

I am sitting here at my desk. A table that was hand-carved by a woman who sculpted the grand figures upon the court house steps, and who was married to my father's friend and business partner. It was perfect while it rested in my father's house, but since it was gifted to me to write upon, puppies have chewed the beautiful legs, and cups have left rings upon its surface. I can never grasp the marring of perfection that so often follows my life. I can feel shame and grief, or I can feel gratitude and thankfulness. I can choose to look long at the scratches and the puppy bites, or I can give thanks for the history and the love that sculpted the legs. I am grateful for the gift. It reminds me of my beloved dad every time I sit here.

He is one of my gifts. He is one of my graces. He is not perfect and neither am I, but he is loved and admired by all who meet him. His spirit emanates God's acceptance. His ability to give is without measure. He is long on this earth and he leaves legacies of grace. One of my greatest joys is bearing witness to my eighty-eight-year-old father putting on his waders and fly fishing. He has been doing it since he was a little boy and it comes as natural to him as his breath. He and the river speak the same language. It was the language taught to my brother and me when we were just tiny. It was the language passed down from my grandfather, and his father before him. I take out my camera and capture the day, watching him, still sure footed in water up to his knees, casting the line. A fisher of men. A fisherman. He wears the same hat his father wore for over a half a century as the sun beat down upon the brim. The sweat of a grandfather, a father, a brother and a sister, stains the cloth with our DNA. "A River Runs Through It." The hat is beyond "ripe", but he and I love it. It will hang on a wall when he has gone. Watching him on the river leaves me all bare, ripe in Gods glory upon *his* created being, my father.

~~~

Giving thanks is what the bible says to do in our lives. "Give thanks in all things." All things Lord? What does that mean? Do you mean give thanks for the pain or the losses or the grief over injustices? How can that message be from a loving God who wants only good things for *his* creation? Can that really be true? All things? So I wring my heart out to dry and I know that I need more Jesus to be able to attempt such an amazing feat in such a troubled and unjust world.

More of God in my life, more of Jesus, more love, more learning how to roll in the deep with the keeper of me, and not struggle. The weight of the waves crashing upon me threaten to crush me. So I keep my eyes on *him*, raise my eyes unto the hills, and know where my help comes from. My help comes from the Lord. Becoming thankful for all things because I gave God my life. My life is *his* to do with as *he* will. To be thankful for all things because thankfulness brings witness to grace and grace brings ease of the assurance that I am in *his* hands. Thankfulness is the key to open me to more grace from God's storehouse of love. It opens the floodgates for the spirit of love to reside in my eyes, that I might see the many gifts *he* has given. From the light upon the wings of a thousand birds landing in an open field, to the droplets of rain on a window pane. In *his* grace, I have eyes to see these things. I have ears to hear. From the gentle snoring of my loved one beside me and the sounds of Mozart in the air where I reside, to the laughter of my father, who is still with me on this earth. I have ears to hear the gifts. To know that my very breath this morning has come from *his* love, and I can know this for certain and feel thankful. I am on a quest to see and taste and smell and hear the grace all around me. To know intimately the hand that feeds me, to hear the voice that gently calls my name in the third watch of the night. I am hunger and I am thirst, and there is no quenching of the fire apart from the grace of thanksgiving. There is no filling of the wine or the breaking of bread inside the challis of my life with *him*, apart from thanksgiving. I see lack, but *he* is plenty. I feel fear, but *he* is faith. I wander and *he* waits. Only the grace of *his* presence restores me to sanity again.

I am thankful this morning for the many gifts of *his* grace. For the wisdom to know that the answer to everything empty and lost, is thanksgiving to the one who brings life and heals wounds and bears sin upon a broken body made whole. I am thankful for the table of love that I will be seated at, with loved ones, new and old, that brings grace into my tempest storms. On this *amazing grace* morning, I raise my eyes to the dawns early light, and see the wonders of the gift and say "Thanks" in the hushed tone of one long waiting for an answer to her pain. It has been there all the time I wandered lost and weary. The answer is thankful. The answer is grace through thanksgiving and the eyes to see *his* love. In every storm and in every barren place, *He* is.

~~~

"Amazing grace how sweet the sound that saved a wretch like me. I once was lost but now I'm found, was blind but now I see." *

~~~

If we are able to receive the falling of the rain, the *Holy Spirit* upon our parched souls, we will very soon have an accumulation of love and grace large enough to water our lands on which we build our lives.

What do I want? For grace to fall upon me like a rainstorm while I, bare foot and wild in the grace, become whole in the message.

Chapter sixteen

Blessings

The morning light
The stars at night
A baby's laugh
A friend's hug
A puppy's tug
The forest's trees
The ocean's breeze
The watch by night
Reconciliation after a fight

Eyes to see
Ears to hear
A voice that speaks
Lavender soap in a jar
A claw foot tub
A hot-water soak
Laughter at someone's joke

A constant voice in my ear

A gentle snore beside me in the bed

Twenty years of walking side by side

A sleigh ride

Winter's white

Silent night

Amazing grace

A Kentucky Derby race

The smells of Christmas

The reason he died

I am blessed

I am blessed

A father's love

For all these years

A brother's life (I miss you still)

A girl who is a family chord

A musical note in the open air

I am blessed

I am blessed

Baby creatures

Dolphins and Butterflies

Birds that sing
A hammock swing
Water from a tap
Doesn't get much better than that.

I can dance and I can sing and I can speak on behalf of innocent things.
I can dream and I can rest and I can ski with some of the best.
I can garden upon my knees and I can grow a beautiful tree.
I can count the times an angel got her wings.
God is a mysterious thing
I am blessed
I am blessed.
There are spaces in the heart
Full of memories torn apart
God was gentle in the storms
I am blessed
I am blessed
Books and poems and grace under pressure
Love and trial without measure.

The Savior knew the story
Before he bled red
And I am fed.
I am blessed.
I am blessed.

Chapter seventeen

I Have Gone Round

The earth is round, and I have traveled, through skies and clouds and rivers wild. I have gone to canyons and into oceans. I have swum with a sea lion and been chased by an otter in playful abandon. I have stepped onto shorelines and sailed on the back of a ray. I climbed, with blisters on my feet, a mountain. I slept with strangers watching over me, and awakened with a friend. I have crested the hill straight into a harvest moon that swallowed me. I have been alone, and I have been surrounded by people. The earth has cried to me loudly for help. The earth has opened wide its splendor. Rain forests and sandy beaches, wayward back roads of dirt and dust. I have seen migrations for miles, swarms of life searching for a home. I have grieved the dying faces and held the hands of those who leave us. I have been flung farther and harder than I ever imagined I could be, from sea to shining sea. I have drunk of the wine and run through the vineyards, covered in peach fuzz and juices. I have been a naked dreamer with a dream. I have carried the sick, and I have been an instrument of peace. I have met those who change the world, and I know that God loved that wino behind the dumpster so deeply I could barely stand upright in the presence of the love. I have fallen more times than I can count, shared my vulnerabilities, worn a shield over my heart, shared my only bread. I have been struck by grace in the most unlikely of places. Counted on people who let me down. I have loved many who did not love me in return. I have ridden horses and run with dogs and been kissed by a whale and rubbed a dolphin. I have lived in so many places.

I awaken each day surprised and thankful for the time. Time has never been promised. I live each day as if it were my last. I learned that lesson young. I live as a child; I live as if I am old. Joy blazes through pain. Until I am called home, the earth is round. I am on a bicycle, a plane, a train, a bus, and my feet. Mostly I walk many miles looking up. I don't know what is coming next, and most days, that makes me smile. I try to stay kind. I don't often succeed, especially when I am bone tired and feeling small. The earth carries me when I have need of grace. The Lord carries the earth. And so we go together, my God and me. Sometimes I am running ahead and I trip and fall. Sometimes I am hiding in God's coat tails feeling very small. Mostly we walk hand in hand. *His,* larger than the universe; and mine, small as a particle. *He* is the roadmap for the whole earth. *He* is the birth place of wonder. Yet I am here to live. The whole of me to live. To want to bring beauty and be beauty, to want to be loved and give love. To grab onto grace and never let go.

The earth is round and on we go...God and this girl. I have a name; that name is child.

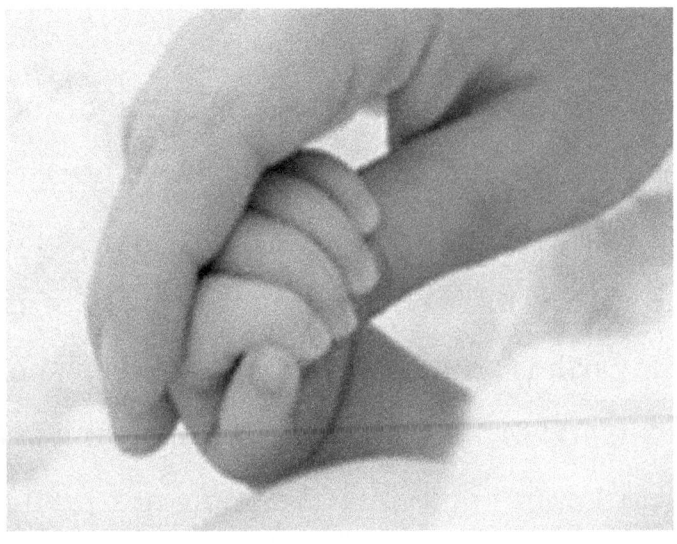

Chapter eighteen

Come Inside

It is October and the garden is turning brown. I am listening to dead leaves under my feet as I walk a now crooked path through the forest. The apples never came this year thanks to the early storms beating the flowers off the trees. I am wrapped up in scarves from generations before me. A grandmother passed it to my mother, who passed it to me. I search for the scent of one who combed my hair and scrutinized my dress every morning before school. She has been gone two years now. Since I have suffered so many deaths close together, I feel like we are running out of time. There is a sense of urgency in my soul. The historical clock is ticking loudly as well. The battle lines are being drawn in the sand. The hour glass is running out. We are being asked to follow *him* up the hill carrying the cross. *His* people are dying in the Middle East for their faith. Most of us are not strong enough to look evil in the eye with love in our hearts. Most of us are lukewarm, we sit our bodies down on a Sunday and we say our prayers and sing our hymns and yet we can't overcome anything. We live in our warm bath water of indifference and we don't make any change in the world. God doesn't need us, but *he* looks for hearts that need *him* and *he* draws near enough to breathe life into our lukewarm souls and kindles a fire so that we carry *him* to the world. When I can do this, grace swoops in, lifts me up and carries the love in the state of grace. Whether I am wandering in the wilderness, or watching the red moons, or on a mission for love, I am not my own. *He* is me and I am *he*. We are one truth. The whole of me is a molecular wonder of GOD-like particles, willing to be released. Like a balloon let go to fly. If I am willing I can give my heart. Daily, release it into *his* heart and become the lesson. Fly on wings that cannot be seen. Trust the journey, even in one of pain or sickness. When the storms come in wild fury, I can know that *he* will lead me home. Home is *his* heart. Home is *him*. The God-sized hole in all of us, that only *he* can fill. There isn't any other taste that will satisfy. I can choose to remember that God does not cause our suffering. That *he* carries the suffering in *his* God sized hand, if we let *him*. I can remind myself that heaven will one day come to me, and all of us who know *him*, but for now *he* winks in the stars and caresses me under the moon with *his* love. *He* shows himself in the morning light and the birds in flight. *He* shows himself when a baby is born or a loved one dies. I can remind myself that in heaven there are many rooms and one day *he* will carry me home. I can almost hear *him* say as *he* opens *his* arms to let me in "Come inside, lay your burdens down." *He* is the love that calls gently to all of us to come inside. Come inside *his* heart, come inside *his* words, come inside *his* mystery, and come inside *his* grace. Just come.

Chapter Nineteen

Beauty for Ashes

My husband comes out of the shower smelling like spring. The sun rises amongst the forest trees, where sparrows are eating from the red feeder hanging in the bird sanctuary we created, to give them shelter, a feeder and a bath. I am embracing my life. I am hugging the joy up against my skin and feel life returning to my soul. In the middle of my earth shifting, I am sensing God restoring what is broken and I am hearing the notes of angels floating in the air. The toast pops up and the puppies are wrestling under my feet as the aroma of cinnamon and oatmeal comes to beckon a once wayward appetite. I am putting weight on again. All is being restored. There is something so holy in restoration. Something so beautiful in the quiet simple ways of my life. I am learning to celebrate simple things, learning to love all the mysteries, the changing colors from within as I walk in the woods and sit on a swing. I will pump my legs and lean back, looking straight up into the blue sky, with my mouth wide open and full of wonder, in this moment of pure joy, soaring like a child. I am learning to let the wind whip my hair off my face and not be anxious in the strong light with all my imperfections revealed. I am learning to embrace the imperfections of me. I am growing old and yet I am feeling young again. I am exploring all the wonders that are beckoning me, learning to let go of the rope that has tethered me to fear, whether to free fall or fly into my days, trusting at long last, that the God who made me, who has kept me and carried me through fires and floods, will never leave me. Trusting in the end that all is love. Trusting in the end that all is grace. Because *He* is the *Keeper of me*.

Acknowledgments

One of the best parts of writing a book is thanking those people for whom I am most grateful. There have been many along the way.

First to those who have helped me with kindness and shelter across the many years of wandering to find my home.

Phil and Marianne Wood, for opening your arms and your home to me after the poisons came.

Paige and Greg Evans, who have sheltered me with their love for over 38 years.

Jary Daily, my mentor in the beginning of my journey, when I was most afraid.

Carolyn McDonald Anna, for a season of the most comfortable bed I have ever laid my head.

Those who helped me with my orphan work by lending me your skills and your hearts to help others less fortunate:

Victoria Woodworth, Joe Schriner, John Reece, Dan Oertli, Jim Benneman, Paige Evans and William Alspaugh, Aaron Wagner, Randy Sabados and Tim Hubler. Roger Ward for your line editing, this is a much better book because of you. John Blasé, an amazing poet and writer himself, thank you for your words and thoughts and to Autumn Shields and Joe Schriner for your editing time. Thank you, Elizabeth Presb. Church (Elizabeth, Co.), Priest Lake Pres. Church (Nashville, Tenn.), Corona Presb. Church (Denver, Co), Lowell Tursick, Tawnie (The artist), Life Outreach, Jesus Alive and all of you who have given to me over the years to help me fund what will as of this writing, be our 16th water well.

I wish to thank those who have prayed for me over the years and those who have encouraged me along the way. Victoria Woodworth, John Reece, Joe Schriner, Paige Evans, Jary Daily, Hannah Griffith, Julie Baggett, Cat Russell, Autumn Shields, JoAnn Hall, Nora and Derwin Bohne, and Nancy Carlson, who was grace one desperate day. To my sweet neighbor Sheila Stone, I miss our fence time. To Thurston who is a tattered angel. To my new neighbors who are bringing me a fresh energy and love to my broken heart. Liz Calvert and your Sammy, Diana and Kevin Pollard. Thank you to the village I now call home, the gentle energy from the people who live here and the forest that has sheltered me and is restoring my soul.

To the Facebook friends, I feel like I know. Thank you for being there for me with kindness and prayers, cards and phone calls: Kelly O'Dell Stanley, Susy Paris, Wes McIntyre, John Breckenridge, Sue Ellen Trout, Joanna Merrick, Sheryle Hensley and Rose Schings.

To Friendships from long ago who sneak in to my life just enough to stay a part of my tribe. (You know who you are) especially Emily Bush and Geno Sack, Dave, Sue and Lela Peters, Janet Groom.

To Steven and Annie Brooks and Anne Edstrom. My dearest Uncle Derry, who is always a gentle man to me. To Victoria Woodworth who is in every stitch of my tapestry, my heart is so thankful. There is none like you. When God put us together thirty-eight years ago he wasn't kidding. You are the sister I never had.

To John Reece who is a lot of grace and laughter and love. I am blessed beyond measure to call you Dad. You inspire me to be a better person and you are the kindest person I know.

Joe my sweet and tenacious husband who took me on twenty years ago and never let me go. Thank you for having my back and supporting my passions. You are my helpmate and my friend. Thank you for helping me always with everything in my life. You are something very special.

This whole book is for you *God* the Father, *God* the Son and *God* the Holy one.... I am quite the stubborn child. I love you so much and I am really thankful that you see me and love me just the way I am. You will always be the keeper of me Lord. I couldn't do anything apart from you, except get lost.

Notes

Orphan work.

To donate or find ways to help the orphans

www.drlynnandtheorphans.com

Hear the music and contact information.

www.lynnschriner.com

lynnschriner@gmail.com

Come Inside Producer/Engineer/Instrumentalist Aaron Wagner

Written by Victoria Woodworth. Vocals Lynn Schriner

Red Blood moon from a sermon by Bob Beltz. September 20, 2015

Photo credits

Cover Unknown (Public domain)

Moon and stars (Public domain)

Amazing Grace (Public domain)

All other photos (Lynn Schriner)

Moon shot (Public domain)

Lynn and the puppies (Joe Schriner)

Back cover photo and arms up photo (Sarah Cutright)

Michael Collopy is the author of Architects of Peace & Works of Love are works of peace.

2-4-D is a derivative of Agent Orange. Roundup was one of the poisons that almost took my life. Monsanto, Bayer, Johnson & Johnson, Dow chemicals are all responsible for spraying and dumping nearly 160 billion pounds of poisons into our soil, water and air each year. It is NOT safe and it is slowly killing us all. I stand with those who fight them. Earth Justice, Millions against Monsanto, Erin Brockovich and Pesticide Action Network (PAN.) My hope is that you will get involved and change your own use of chemicals. We have babies and grandbabies to think of. Every generation is getting sicker. Cancer is rampant. We may live longer than our ancestors but the quality of our health is poor. Most people don't feel well. They are tired, or depressed, or have chronic health issues that no one knows why. I believe it is the chemicals that are overloading our systems. We must **not** vote for those who vote to protect the chemical companies. Do your homework please. There is still time if we stand up and say, "NO More."

Bible References*

This is my comfort and my consolation in my affliction: that your word has revived me and given me life Psalms 119:50

The Lord is the same yesterday, today and forever more. Hebrews 13:8

The Lord giveth and the Lord taketh away and blessed be the name of the Lord.

What do you want with us Jesus of Nazareth? Mark 5:7

The peace that surpasses all understanding Philippians 4:7

Parting of the Red Sea. Exodus 14:21-27

Prophesy to these dry bones Ezekiel 37:4

Praise the Lord in all things 1 Thessalonians 5:18

Yea, thou you walk through the valley of the shadow of death Psalms 23

Faith is the substance of things not seen Hebrews 11:1

For God so loved the world that he gave his only begotten son that whosoever believes in him shall not perish but have ever lasting life. John 3:16

But we believe -are saved through grace Acts 15:11

After Notes

On October 16th Damascus Ministries/Dr. Lynn & the orphans, funded our 15th water well for orphans on the continent of Africa, with the help of Life Outreach International and Jesus Alive.

This book and the song Come Inside will be assisting in the funding of our subsequent water projects.

Download the song from my Band camp page:
https://www.lynnschriner1.bandcamp.com/

To all of the orphans in my heart I want to share this beautiful work by Nancy Tillman from "On the Night You Were Born"

On the night you were born,
The moon smiled with such wonder,
That the stars peeked in to see you
And the night wind whispered, "Life will never be the same."
Because there has never been anyone like you...
Ever in the world.
Heaven blew every trumpet
And played every horn on the wonderful, marvelous night you were born.

Venus and the moon

They hang like earthly friends in a cosmos sky

Dancing in God's creation of light

The sounds of Brahms lullaby

Within their ears

Sharing the wonder of the universe

In this galaxies so bright

They are content to be brilliant

Just by hanging together

On the star's corner of infinity

God's splendor…Good night sweet friends

Lynn and her puppies
The Cottage 2015

www.ingramcontent.com/pod-product-compliance
Lightning Source LLC
Chambersburg PA
CBHW051652040426
42446CB00009B/1099